CARDIFF: HALF

*Series Editor*: MEIC STEPHENS

# Cardiff:
# half-and-half a Capital

## Rhodri Morgan

First Impression—May 1994

ISBN 1 85902 112 3

Printed in Wales by
J. D. Lewis, and Sons Ltd., Gomer Press, Llandysul, Dyfed

What would Cardiff's football team be called if we adopted the American habit of naming it after the main industry of the area? Come to think of it, that's one of the few things the USA and the USSR had in common—they thought their big cities were best defined by their major industries, the ones that put them on the map in the first place.

The sports team that represented the city to the outside world therefore had to follow suit: Moscow Dynamo, Pittsburgh Steelers, Lokomotiv Leningrad, Houston Oilers, Detroit Pistons, San Francisco '49ers, and so on. Indeed, the manager of the New York Mets baseball team was recently reported to have been so annoyed at the team's lack of the Never Say Die spirit—their habit of giving up altogether when losing in the second half of the game—that he suggested they should all emigrate to the Philipines: they could then be re-named the Manila Folders! There's nothing quite so brutal as American baseball managers' humour.

If it were a British custom, what would Cardiff's football team be called, and would it give a clue about the kind of city Cardiff is? The short-lived Rugby League team sort of went for the American habit, but only halfway. They plumped for Cardiff Blue Dragons. If that choice of name is spot on, it tells you that the only thing that defines Cardiff, that gives the city 'a touch of class' in the eyes of the world, is being the capital of Wales. The Dragons had to be blue because the municipal coat·of arms is blue, as befits a seaport. Otherwise it would be Red Dragons like everything else in Wales.

But Cardiff is much more than just the capital of Wales. It is a city in its own right and not an artificial creation like Canberra or Ottawa. What put Cardiff on the map before its relatively recent designation as capital? The more recent and much more success-ful ice-hockey team has gone for the name-tag of Devils. They play well enough but 'Devils'? Devils could be associated with any place at all. Why Devils or alternatively, why Cardiff? It's not even trying to get close to the soul of the city, which at least the name of Dragons did.

Calling a Cardiff sports team the Dragons is like calling the Cardiff concert hall St. David's Hall; the same goes for the covered shopping-centre behind Queen Street and Working Street. Why not call it the Captain Morgan Centre, after Henry Morgan the pirate? Dewi Sant may be the patron saint of Wales and Cardiff its capital, but consider the case for Captain Morgan (and he's no relation of mine).

Henry Morgan was born in Llanrumney, and his name is better-known around the world than any other native of Cardiff, even if for mostly the wrong reasons. Property developers and chain-store owners aren't exactly pirates, but they surely behave more like them than like early Celtic saints.

Then take the concert hall. Why not call it the Novello Hall? I'm no fan of Ivor Novello's music, but he's probably Cardiff's only significant contribution to the world of music. What is more, he's the only person born and raised in the city deemed famous enough to have a blue plaque on the wall of the house where he was brought up in Riverside. So why exactly didn't the city fathers call it the Ivor Novello Concert Hall?

Better still, why not the Bassey-Novello Hall? Perhaps including a mention of 'our Shirl' in the title of the city's concert hall would have bestowed too much of a 'pop' image for the taste of Cardiff's Establishment, musical and otherwise. But isn't it just a touch boring to call all these grand new landmarks in our city after Wales' patron saint? Christening one St. David's development would have been enough. Two shows Cardiff's lack of self-confidence in its own home-grown status as a city, when removed from its pedestal as 'capital of Wales'.

Maybe Brent Walker, the owners of the new giant 5,000-seat auditorium in the World Trade Centre on Bute Terrace, can put this omission right in 1994, now that it has finally opened its doors after an elephantine gestation period. They have renamed the whole building the Cardiff International Arena, or CIA for short. If they were to call the auditorium the Bassey-Novello Hall, it would fix it well and truly in the heart of the city. It would also identify it clearly on the musical map of the world.

Perhaps what we now need is a statutory limit to the number of times Cardiff can call on its 'Welsh Capital' status in naming its 'trophy' developments. I have nothing against Welsh patriotism, nationhood, or Cardiff's status as a capital city. It's just that I don't think that the people in charge of choosing these 'capital of Wales'-type names so repetitively did so out of Welsh patriotism or respect for early British Christianity.

They chose and re-chose St. David this and Red Dragon that because it was safe, bland and reassuring and therefore dead right in modern marketing terms. It was the acceptable face of Welsh nationhood, and not a threat to anyone. It is a quiescent assertion of passive nationhood without the national or civic pride. You may be in Wales but really it's no different from Milton Keynes, so you don't have to worry about it. So much for Wales and so much for Cardiff!

What I would prefer to see just occasionally is that we give names to our prestige buildings which might inspire young people with self-confidence about their city—or which offered role-models for their own aspirations. The citizens of Cardiff have suffered suffocation with a blanket of uniform and bland symbolism, one which shuts them out. Cardiff exists not just to be capital of Wales but to develop its own personality as well. It's the powers-that-be in Cardiff who suffer from that lack of pride in being Cardiffian, and not its citizens.

What about these citizens? If they were given the chance, what name would they choose for their concert hall or shopping-centre or football-team to represent them to the rest of the world? What makes, or at least at one time made, Cardiff famous? Is there anything that we are Number One City for? What industry do we lead in, or more exactly did we lead in, before the relentless rise and rise of Japan and Taiwan. What's the real Cardiff equivalent of the Pistons of Detroit, the Oilers of Houston and the Dynamos of Moscow?

Years ago it would have perhaps been the Cardiff Coal-Trimmers, or maybe the Cardiff Re-Rollers or Iron-Puddlers. With the overlay of Inland Revenue and public administration that arrived in and after the Second World War, the character of the city has changed hugely. Could a team realistically be called the Cardiff Taxers and run out onto a field full of the old gung-ho 'We'll take on the world' feeling? Perhaps not.

Recently I saw a helpful suggestion in this area of philosophical inquiry in Gren's strip-cartoon on life in the rugby-obsessed Valleys. The match notice on the clubhouse wall for the following Saturday's big game indicated that the local heroes, Aberflyarff RFC, were entertaining 'Cardiff Quangos Third XV'! If the main occupation that defines working life in Cardiff isn't working for the Revenue or one of the Welsh Office Quangos, then what is it? If the Pittsburgh Steelers, then how about the Cardiff Double-Glazing Sales Reps? The Cardiff Management Consultants? Would the people of the city come along and cheer?

## WHY THE RADYR LOCOS NEVER CAME BACK

I'm interested because, although I was born in Connaught Road in the Roath district of the city, I was raised in Radyr. The village was not a part of the city then, but was later incorporated within the city limits. As I was born in 1939, I was six when the war ended and Radyr's famed (to us villagers) pre-war football team, the Radyr Locos, never re-formed after 1945. That was a tragedy for our village because the Locos defined it—both the engines and the team.

So you see: there was one place in Wales which did believe in calling its favourite sports team after its biggest, or in Radyr's case, its only industry. After the war, standing on a street-corner doing nothing in particular was known in Radyr as 'waiting for the Radyr Locos to come back'. The Locos were almost our only claim to fame and we'd lost them. Our only other trophy was the holy well of Pistyll Goleu, or Pitchicoola, as we called it in our local dialect.

Unlikely though it may seem to any observer now, looking at the acres of new housingestates with acres of white Hygena kitchen units to match, which surround the old village, Radyr in the 1940s and 1950s was not all that bad a microcosm of the

Cardiff that engulfed it in the 1970s. The bottom end was dominated by the giant sidings—the marshalling yards for all the coal-trains from the Valleys waiting to be distributed to the Docks, or sometimes to Barry or the power-stations.

Only Clapham Junction had bigger sidings, we were always taught in the village primary school (or maybe it was with our mothers' milk). Yes, we were taught to boast to anyone who would listen that our railway sidings were the biggest in Britain after Clapham Junction! Now that the marshalling-yards have been closed and are about to be sold for yet more housing-estates, what will they be teaching children to boast about in the village school? Not, I hope, that Radyr has more Hygena kitchens to the square mile than any other place on earth.

The top of the village near the golf-course was dominated by the big houses of the coal-owners, plus some of the 'new people' who owned the factories on the Treforest Trading Estate. In the middle, somewhere between the railway workers' families and the coal-owners, were the BBC and University people like us Morgans.

The BBC and University people were mostly Welsh-speaking and, in the 1950s and 60s, upwardly mobile. Not so much the intelligentsia as the in-telly-Welshia. As they went up in the world, they passed coming down another significant group in the Radyr of those days—those who claimed to be 'something on the Docks'.

To be 'something on the Docks' had once been a real sign of status in Cardiff life. It was something you boasted about to the neighbours or to prospective in-laws. It was a grown-up equivalent of our claim that Radyr had the biggest sidings after Clapham Junction. By the 1950s it actually meant that you'd had very little to do since about 1925—apart from boasting perhaps.

The decline of the coal-trade burghers of Radyr, who even then hadn't done any serious burghing for over twenty-five years and who thus had remarkably low golf-handicaps, and the giant railway sidings with its engine turntable I loved to watch, these were my first introduction, my windows onto the economic foundation-stones of Cardiff's rise and fall. You couldn't live in

Radyr and fail to hear the hooters. You couldn't live in Radyr and not be aware that Cardiff was originally built on the export of coal from the Valleys, because Radyr was too. Nor could you possibly be unaware that a glorious past was no guarantee to the city's economic future.

The Radyr Locos never came back and neither did the coal export trade. For some, the compensation was whiling away every afternoon on the golf-course getting your handicap down; for others it was quietly polishing off a daily bottle of gin in the study. Their economic *raison d'être* had disappeared from under them. These days it's not just a matter of waiting for the Radyr Locos football team to come back. It will very shortly be waiting for the Radyr Loco Sheds themselves to come back, and it's a Mickey Thomas fiver to the entire contents of Fort Knox that they never will. If Max Boyce had come from Radyr and not Glynneath, the words of his ballad would not be 'The pithead bath's a supermarket now' but rather, 'There are wall-to-wall Hygena Kitchens now, where the shunters used to hoot'.

Gold-rush mining camps in Alaska or Nevada just became ghost-towns when the gold ran out. The same has fortunately not happened to the South Wales coalfied, nor to the Valleys where the miners lived, nor to Radyr where the coalowners and the shunters lived either. Nor did Cardiff itself die. It became a capital city instead.

Now that we have lost the last pit in the Valleys, and the steel industry in Cardiff only employs two-thousand people, is this perhaps the right time to re-evaluate Cardiff and its place in Welsh life? How did it get to be Wales' largest city? How did it get to be the capital? Does it do the job that the rest of Wales really requires of a capital city? Does Cardiff fertilize or strangulate the life of Wales? Does being the capital fertilize or strangulate the life of the city itself? What sort of capital for what sort of country?

There are no objective answers to these questions—which is just as well since, like everyone else, I can only give strictly personal answers. The five decades that I've lived in and around Cardiff don't qualify me to say too much too authoritatively about all the other decades nor about all the other neighbour-hoods and lifestyles that I've never experienced directly myself.

Although brought up in a semi-detached in Radyr, I've never felt semi-detached about Cardiff. The proportions of rich, middling and poor were quite different in Radyr from the body of the city proper, yet the experience of life was parallel. To be lulled to sleep every night by the hooters of the shunting engines, blended with the noise of the inky waters of the Taff tumbling over Radyr Weir, gave me contact with the magic ingredients that made Cardiff originally spring to life as a city. That is my perspective.

## THE MISSING PAGES

To me it is very fitting that the only historic figure from Cardiff whose name is known throughout the world should be a pirate—a pirate furthermore, who halfway through his swash-buckling lifetime joined the Establishment just to keep historians guessing about whose side he was on. Captain Henry Morgan may have got the royal appointment to become Governor of Jamaica late in life, but his fame is based on the earlier buccaneer part of his career. It poses the obvious question. Are we Cardiffians pirates or are we Establishment?

Our pre-industrial history is very Establishment. Cardiff started life as a Roman fortress and Anglo-Norman garrison-town. It was the best place for fording the river Taff for troops moving east and west across the South Wales plain. Even today the centre of the city is physically dominated by the castle, with its Roman base and Norman keep. What you see today is what's left. What is left, that is, of what the ancient and mediaeval powers-that-were created. There were plenty of bandits and pirates around as well and not all concentrated up around Caerphilly and Senghennydd. You cannot today see our bandit inheritance. There is no way of looking at the ruins and seeing Owain Glyndŵr sacking the castle. Ancient monuments, by their very nature, cannot help over-emphasizing the Establishment version of history. Cardiff is a classic example of that.

Most of all, as you walk around the city centre, what you see is the Marquis of Bute's nineteenth-century reconstruction of the outer walls. It's unusual, really, for a captain of industry to want to rebuild a mediaeval castle for a family home in the centre of an expanding city. Perhaps it was a mistake for the Bute family as well. That may be why he became bored with just one castle in Cardiff. He then went on to build his 'second home' castle on the south face of the Taff Gorge above Tongwynlais with views over the coastal plain, the last six or seven miles of the length of the Taff Vale and its estuary, the Channel and in between the two, the expanse of Cardiff itself.

When Cardiff reached its industrial and commercial heyday in the second half of the nineteenth century, it was emphatically not a place you could call a city. It was just a company-town belonging to the Marquis of Bute. It could not be compared with Bristol at that period in the diversity and depth of trade, its merchants and politicians, or in the number of 'movers and shakers'. There was only one 'mover and shaker' in Cardiff and that was the Marquis: if he said 'Jump!', the only question you asked was, 'How high?'

How did the Marquis' company-town become the capital city of Wales? Maybe that transition was not such an extraordinary jump, after all. First the city belongs lock, stock and barrel to the Marquis, then soon after it belongs to Wales. The problem for Cardiff is this: when did it have a chance to belong to itself like other 'normal' cities? Was that transition from company-town to capital simply too easy? Did we miss out on something vital, something healthy for civic consciousness? Is that the reason for the obsession with St. David's this and Red Dragon that in today's Cardiff? Are we too ready to accept all the restrictions and obligations that go with being a capital city, because Cardiff has never been used to being its own boss?

The other part of the answer may lie in how and why Cardiff's history seems to have 'stopped' after its settlement by the

Romans and the Normans—'stopped', that is, until it became the Marquis of Bute's private fiefdom a century and a half ago.

Like most other middle-sized English, Scottish or European cities, Cardiff seems to have had an important ancient and mediaeval history. It also experienced a typically British nineteenth-century leap forward into the Industrial Revolution and headlong commercial development. Unlike most European cities, however, there is nothing in the middle with Cardiff. It's an almighty leap from '1066 and All That' into the Bute West Dock! You can almost say that Cardiff rose without trace in the 1840s.

Where is the 'old quarter' of Cardiff? There isn't really one at all. Almost none but not quite. The little district, more a 'sixteenth' than a 'quarter', with its narrow streets around St. John's Church, the front of the Castle and down to the old course of the Taff at Quay Street, saves Cardiff from this 'rose without trace' accusation. If you include Llandaf and the neighbourhood around the Cathedral Green, you have just two small areas which remind you of pre-industrial but urban Cardiff.

If it wasn't for these half-a-dozen streets, Cardiff's character and appearance would be much more like an American city founded no earlier than the nineteenth century than a 'normal' European city. Normal European capitals have an 'Old Quarter' with winding alleyways and half-timbered merchants' houses opening out onto Georgian squares (or their equivalents) in which markets are held every other Wednesday when gnarled old craftsmen and costerwomen sell hand-made chocolates, lace or musical boxes, or whatever the local speciality is.

Cardiff just doesn't have anything like that. You can't sell forty-foot-long steel billets to tourists. The only equivalent to a local speciality that I can think of is bakestones. There was a foundry in Cardiff which used to manufacture special bakestones for making Welsh cakes, whenever they had some molten material left over. A cast-iron bakestone is hardly the right thing for the casual tourist or shopper to pop into a shoulder-bag, though, is it?

We don't have an old quarter and we don't have historic old crafts to make us world-renowned, like Nottingham's lace and Birmingham's jewellery. It's simply missing from our history. It's missing because pre-industrial Wales was too poor to generate the economic, cultural or political activity and wealth to keep a phone-kiosk busy, let alone a city, even less so a fully-fledged capital city. If the collective efforts of the Welsh could sustain any big city-type activities before 1800, it was done in London, and maybe in Liverpool and Bristol, but not within Wales. Jesus College, Oxford, was Wales' only university, in contrast to Scotland which had four of its own. London was to all intents and purposes the capital of Wales.

The 'feel' of Cardiff today is pre-determined by the Marquis of Bute's iron grip, in both senses, on the city's sudden burst of development in the middle of the last century. He reconstructed the castle; he kept the huge parkland running up the Taff on both banks as his hunting-grounds. He donated the land for the civic centre to be laid in true Imperial style at Cathays Park.

He also brought the architect William Burges to Cardiff to work on the reconstruction of the castle and on scores of other notable buildings. The best of them is perhaps the old Cardiff Rural District Council offices in Park Place. Cardiff would be dominated by the Gothic Revival style of building even if William Burges had never been near the place. He added a little something extra. Every Gothic Revival architect and stonemason likes to put a signature on the face and skyline of a building—a cupola, a carved face or two, the date of construction in elaborate numbering, that was the style. Burges just took it further.

Should we make more fuss of him in Cardiff? Is he to Cardiff what Charles Rennie Mackintosh is to Glasgow? That city has made at least a tourist-industry, if not a religion, out of worshipping Mackintosh. I don't think Burges was quite in the Mackintosh class, but we do seriously undervalue Burges. It is astonishing how difficult it is to get a good understanding of his contribution to the 'feel' of the city we live in. Bringing him to spend most of his adult working-life here was one of the lasting contributions of the Third Marquis.

Let us not forget either that Bute also straightened the course of the river and relocated the docks southward to the sea from their historic location at the upper tidal reach of the Taff, halfway up Westgate Street at its junction with Quay Street in the city centre. I am by no means sure that the Marquis was actually that much of a rugby fanatic. He is though the accidental cause of why Cardiff Arms Park comes to be in the city centre where the river used to wend its way from east to west, while really trying to go south to the sea. When you see some of today's rugby supporters on match day lurching their way down Westgate Street swaying from side to side, all they are doing is trying to follow the winding old course of the Taff, as oblivious to the Marquis of Bute as to everything else. Most cities don't have fifty acres of prime real estate in the city centre devoted to the occasional ten-times-a-year use for two hours on a Saturday afternoon to play or watch rugby. There would be skyscraper offices there, or five-star hotels, or government Ministry buildings. The National Stadium ought to be two or three miles away on the edge of town in strict land economics terms.

The same applies to the huge expanse of parkland extending northward from Bute Park and Cooper's Field just behind the Castle and the Animal Wall up through Sophia Gardens, Pontcanna Fields, Blackweir up to Llandaf Fields. That would be prime real estate too. After all, most of it is within spitting distance of the city centre and much too valuable to be left green. In a typical European city, it would be part of the civic centre, the shopping centre or the commercial centre. It would certainly be built over, with something important, something that added to urban prestige.

There wasn't the pressure to release all that prime central area during the decades of Cardiff's expansion, because commercial offices were not in or near the centre anyway. Cardiff's commercial heart was a mile away in Mountstuart Square in the Docks. When you look at the huge banking halls of the Big Four banks' branches at the Docks end of Bute Street, you realize that these were not branch offices, designed to handle sailors' wages and do the odd bit of foreign currency exchange. These were without question the principal branches, the ones where the big deals were done. In a normal-shaped city those banks would have been located somewhere in the middle of Cardiff Arms Park or behind the Animal Wall in the Castle Grounds. So we have a park in the city centre and our historic financial centre down around the Pier Head. It's not normal, it's not logical, but it is Cardiff.

In the past twenty years there have been proposals to build over both the National Stadium and Bute Park. The scheme to redevelop the Stadium was put forward by the leaders of the County Council at the height of the property boom a couple of years ago. The rugby ground would move three miles west to Leckwith and fifty acres of prime city centre land would then be freed for redevelopment. The scheme for Bute Park involved a new Roman Catholic Cathedral, judges' living quarters and a new home for the Welsh National Opera and a National Theatre. Protests from park-lovers and rugby-lovers scotched both ideas, even before they had got onto the drawing-board. We have grown used to the shape of our city centre, peculiar though it be.

Whether today's citizens think this curious shape of the city's centre is a tribute to the Marquis or not, it could not have developed that way, very low on density and high on greenery, unless it had been the plaything of one man a hundred and fifty years ago. It's the shape of a company-town, skewed to the personal whim of the man and his money who created modern Cardiff.

He didn't make Cardiff the capital of Wales, but it could never have become the capital without Bute. Love him or hate him, and there weren't many who loved him, today's Cardiff still bears his imprint more than anyone else's. What's more, it bears his imprint much more than any other city bears the imprint of any one single human being. No one person should have that much power over a city. Cardiff has been struggling ever since to find the freedom to develop its own personality, to break free of the Marquis' excessive power and influence.

What is truly remarkable is that much of Wales' self-image as a nation rests on being a separate country from England for sporting purposes. Let's face it, Brittany doesn't play against France in football or rugby; Bavaria doesn't play against Germany. Where would we be today if these international matches had not started to be arranged, originally between Scotland and England, but with Wales and Ireland added on for a bit of variety in the 1870s? It follows that the Welsh National Rugby Stadium is very much at the heart of the way in which Cardiff functions as a capital. It also follows that it is very important that the National Stadium is not out in the suburbs but in the city centre. The Stadium could be described as the principal institution of Welsh nationhood. As we are not an independent country, we don't have a National Parliament. Neither do we have our own Royal Family, so we don't need a Royal Palace. We don't have a State Religion, so we don't have a national cathedral.

This concept of Welsh nationhood mainly rests on our rugby team, because we used to be able to assert with some confidence that we were better than the English at rugby until 1980. The evolution of the stadium into being the home for soccer international matches as well has advanced its totemic status in our national life. What has fascinated me has been the views expressed by leading Welsh soccer-players about playing at the Arms Park Stadium. The top Welsh players of the past decade have all come from north-east Wales, the area that is most remote from Cardiff as a capital.

Yet it was Ian Rush, Kevin Ratcliffe, Hughes and Southall who all said most fervently that they felt six inches taller running out in their red jerseys at the National Stadium. They knew it impressed or even overawed foreign players. It was as good as the football stadiums abroad that Wales had to play at. These North Walian star-players were proud to play there, although they were the very ones who might have been expected most to prefer playing at the Racecourse Ground in Wrexham.

Fanatical Nationalists would or should abhor this football jersey nationalism. It's a diversion from the true cause, for them.

For those who want to see Wales an independent country with its own seat and glass of water at the United Nations, they would want people to support Wales for 365 days of the year, not just when they can get a ticket for the match. Football internationals are the opium of the Welsh masses, they say; it's like bread and circuses under the Roman Empire. 'We are going to bomb the National Stadium to smithereens and not play any international matches against England or anyone else until Wales is an independent country', is what they should be saying. There must be one or two nationalists around who do think along those lines, but I have to admit I've never actually met one. So the stadium is here to stay. So it is a good thing that the Marquis straightened out that little stretch of the Taff.

## A MATTER OF GEOGRAPHY

One thing the Marquis of Bute had no control over was the weather. When I was away at University in 1960, I asked an American fellow-student, as one does, to spend the Christmas holidays with us. Through my father's rugby connections down west we managed to get two field tickets to watch Wales play South Africa in pouring rain on the Saturday afternoon. If it had not been a touring team match, it would have been postponed, so torrential was the rain.

By noon on the Sunday after the game, Cardiff Arms Park was under four feet of water. My American friend and I went down to look at the swollen river Taff at Radyr. It wasn't just swollen. The Taff had burst its banks over a five-mile stretch all the way from Radyr Weir down to Riverside. The not long built Gabalfa council estate was awash. Radyr was lucky—cows drowned but it was only the low-lying farmland and the cricketfield (the previous football field to which the Radyr Locos never did come back) which went under water. I will never forget standing on the railway embankment looking down on the Taff in full spate— the Taff pretending it was the Amazon and the Nile rolled into one, if only for a few days.

To understand Cardiff, you have to know three simple facts about its geographical position entirely beyond the influence of any Marquis. The first is that it lies south of the South Wales coalfield plateau and the Brecon Beacons. The second is that the three rivers which tumble into the Channel at Cardiff drain off the plateau or the southern edge of the Beacons. The longest river, the Taff, is no Amazon: its total length is thirty-five miles. The Rhymney to the east and the Ely to the west are shorter still. Cardiff is built between those three river estuaries. In fact, if it were in Quebec and not Wales, I would lay a bet that the city would be called Trois Rivières. If it were in the American West, it would be called Fort Taff. Funnily enough, that's exactly what it is called, when Caerdaf is translated into English. If it were in Australia, I reckon it would be called Pitchicoola Springs, but then I'm biased coming from Radyr.

The Taff has an importance way beyond its length and catchment area. To English people, we Welsh are known as Taffies or Taffs. Why? Even North Walians who have never seen the inky waters or the plastic-bag-strewn banks of the Taff are known as Taffs. We Southerners might call them Gogs, but we are all Taffs to the English. If the name had become popular in London and the British Armed Forces in the last two centuries, it could be more easily understood. Industrial South Wales had by then become dominant in Welsh life, and the Taff basin could be said to represent the whole of Wales to the outside world.

The expression 'Taffs' goes back to Elizabethan times, however. Londoners began using it when the Welsh started to show up in numbers in London, drawn there by the mistaken belief that the Royal House of Tudor's Welsh connections would guarantee them a job at court. The Taff was just a fishing river of no economic importance. Why aren't we known as Uskies, Teifis, Tywis or Conwys? They are much bigger rivers. They had more fish in them, and bigger harbours.

There is an alternative theory: it is a coincidence that the English name for us, which in fact arises from the mispronunciation of the name Dafydd, sounds like the name of the river Taff. If the name does come from the river, it was

19

certainly an odd choice, but not an impossible one. Maybe the Usk was regarded as not Welsh enough, because it was largely a Monmouthshire river, and that county was not properly part of Wales at the time. Maybe the Teifi, Tywi and Conwy were too far west to be familiar to Londoners. I still find it strange that the English opted for Taffs as the collective name equivalent to 'Wogs' and 'Wops' for us all. Of all the river-names in all of Wales, and they had to dive into this one. Whether the Dafydd theory or the river theory is right, it is mighty convenient that the river of the capital city is the same as the friendly term of abuse for us Welsh.

To form the five-mile-long flood-lake of the river Taff which I goggled at in 1960, the National Rivers Authority has now calculated that the Taff was flowing on that day at a rate of 900 cubic metres per second. That's more than the river Severn has ever discharged in full spate. The Severn is over 240 miles long and drains a huge area of Central Wales and Midlands England. How can the Taff—only thirty-five miles long and with a summer flow of only 3 cubic metres per second—possibly have a higher maximum flow than the Severn which is seven times longer? The answer lies in the Brecon Beacons, one of the world's wettest mountain ranges.

As those Atlantic depressions roll in from the Gulf Stream, the intensity of the rainfall on the Beacons beggars belief. It's not for nothing that the SAS send their raw recruits to the Beacons on survival courses. Why do they deposit young men on a mountain-top in a string-vest with fifty pence and tell them they've got to get to Portsmouth in 48 hours? The regiment simply wants to test its soldiers' ability to survive the wind, the occasional sub-zero temperatures and, above all, that rain. When it feels like half the Gulf of Mexico has been tipped over you, you either survive, realizing that there is little more frightening in the universe, or you are overwhelmed by your own insignificance in the face of Mother Nature at her most vindictive.

When it pours down in the Beacons, that rain is in Cardiff Bay two days later. With these long rivers like the Severn, Wye and Thames, it's at least a fortnight from source to sea. The Taff in spate, shooting all the bridges in Cardiff, looks like a river being chased by the SAS!

The Ely was also known for frequent flooding, although not devastating a great expanse of Cardiff since 1928. That was the flood when the Ely washed eastward across Victoria Park and Canton. Apart from its effects on houses and possessions, it had the odd side-effect of giving a brief taste of freedom to Billy the Seal, the most famous children's pet in Cardiff's history. He normally inhabited the lake in Victoria Park. When the rivers met, he floated or swam as far as Canton Bridge. He then had to be brought home on the platform of a corporation bus. Local myth has it that the conductor gave him a Park Drive cigarette to smoke, to help him enjoy the return journey.

The last unique geographical feature of the city is the huge tidal range, a freak by-product of the funnel shape of the upper Bristol Channel. No other urban area anywhere in the world has a tidal range like Cardiff's 40 feet. The Bay of Fundy in Nova Scotia and some other remote inlet in the Canadian Arctic have a higher rise and fall, but there is no big city on the Bay of Fundy. Cardiff and Newport actually live side by side and tide by tide with 5 cubic kilometres of water sweeping up and down the Channel every 12 hours.

The Taff, the Rhymney and the Ely have brought a lot of mud down into the estuaries over the centuries. Not all of the mud washed out into the Channel; some of it stuck. Cardiff is built on those mudbanks. If the Welsh are sometimes described as the Irish who couldn't swim, then Cardiff might be described as built on the mud that couldn't swim! The old city sat on a pancake made out of mud. To the consternation of visitors who have been told that Wales is nothing but hills, old Cardiff, the pre-First World War city, is much more Dutch than Welsh in landscape and drainage.

From Rumney Hill in the east to Leckwith Hill in the west, there is nothing even resembling a molehill. On the way east from the Taff to the Rhymney, you have the most evocatively named inner city suburb in the world—Splott. That wondrous name is supposed to be an onomatopoeic approximation of the noise your boots made squelching across the boggy terrain. When the mighty Third Marquis started developing housing on the marshes between the Taff and the Ely in the middle part of the last century, the few marsh-dwellers who were already living there frequently suffered from the ague, a benign version of malaria. There was no doubt a lot of 'splotting' across the marshes west of the Taff as well. The whole area was criss-crossed with Dutch polder-type drainage channels to dry out high tides and swollen rivers.

Cardiff people are stubbornly unsentimental about their city's peculiarities—it's their home after all, not some estate agent's PR blurb in a glossy brochure. When the old family home of Ephraim Turner, the founder of Cardiff's best-known building firm, was redeveloped into a trendy tavern some twenty years ago on the banks of the Taff in Grangetown, it was named The Inn on the River. Nothing particularly pretentious about that, you might think—but it wasn't unpretentious enough for the people of Cardiff. It was immediately and permanently re-christened The Pub on the Mud! After all, if a pub looks across at a large iron-foundry, why pretend it's looking across at St. Paul's Cathedral? That renaming by the people was an archetypal Cardiff struggle for supremacy between the smart and the down-to-earth. That's why I refuse to believe rumours about yuppies moving into Splott and wanting to pronounce it Splow with a silent t. It somehow doesn't sound right to say, 'The t is silent as in Splott'.

It is not only the lack of hills that surprises the English visitor fed on *How Green was my Valley*, it is the lack of coalmines as well. The nearest you could get to the mining industry was the distant view of the top of the slag-heap of Bedwas Colliery from high ground on Rumney Hill on the eastern edge of the city. There was also iron-mining on the Little Garth above Morganstown, right on the city's northern limits, but that's about all there has ever been of mining in Cardiff.

Coal and iron and early Industrial Revolution only came to affect Cardiff as by-products of the frantic pace of development going on to the north of the city up on the South Wales plateau.

They did not affect Cardiff directly, nor did they devastate the Cardiff terrain above or below ground. Because there never were any mines or slagheaps in Cardiff it is not unknown for people in the Valleys to say that Cardiff therefore had the easy pickings.

If, however, you were an Irish navvy excavating the Bute East Dock in the 1840s and a refugee from the Potato Famine, I doubt very much if 'easy pickings' was a thought that would have crossed your mind. Nonetheless, the Valleys produced the mineral wealth of South Wales directly by pick and shovel. Cardiff, like Swansea and Newport, got their wealth more indirectly by trade. The relationship between Cardiff and the East Glamorgan Valleys is a delicate one, both politically, historically and economically.

People in the Valleys do understand, I believe, that there were untold thousands in Cardiff who laboured as they did in similar poverty and danger, though above ground. What is perhaps resented is the evolution of a merchant-class in the three main ports and especially in the Coal Exchange in Cardiff 'who made their living off the backs of the miners'. This idea of the interdependence of the Valleys and the city of the plain can stretch very thin at times.

Most big cities have a core of dense urban population. It thins out into the suburbs, then out into the smaller half-rural villages; then it's out to the real farmland. Cardiff is an exception to this pattern. There are more people living in the outer·circle some ten to twenty miles outside Cardiff, than in the inner circle, even though the inner circle includes the city itself. Once you are outside that ten-mile radius, you reach Newport, Pontypridd and the Valleys, Barry to the south-west and Bridgend to the west.

The prosperity or lack of it in this hinterland is what determines the prosperity of the city. What Cardiff really has to watch out for in the future is the suburbanization of the Green Belt area that lies halfway between the outer edge of the city proper and the lower limits of the mining valleys. Rather than filling up that countryside with Wimpey estates, we would do better to preserve the 'hand and fingers' settlement pattern that keeps Cardiff as Cardiff and the Valleys as the Valleys. We do not want a mish-mash, a characterless suburban sprawl.


## MERTHYR'S TRADING-POST

I once heard the Olduvai Gorge in the Serengeti National Park in Tanzania described as the Grand Canyon of Human Evolution. If that's a fair description, then the twenty-four miles of the Taff Vale from Merthyr to Cardiff via Pontypridd could be called the Grand Canyon of the Industrial Revolution. The weaving-towns of Lancashire and West Yorkshire have a strong claim to originating modern mechanization. Some might argue that Coalbrookdale and the Severn Gorge in Shropshire was where the Industrial Revolution really began and maybe it was. But Coalbrookdale never evolved into a town dominated by industrial mass-production as Merthyr did.

That is why Coalbrookdale is such a wonderful museum of the early Industrial Revolution and why Merthyr isn't. The Welsh town will fight like hell against becoming a museum, in spite of its major contribution to the world's industrial history. There are too many people living there now who are looking for an industrial present and future ever to let the place become a museum. They still want mass-production jobs in Merthyr and not jobs in an industrial heritage theme-park.

Without the coal and iron of the South Wales coalfield plateau, Cardiff would have remained a backwater, maybe a sea-trout and salmon-fishing harbour. Without the coal and iron, Wales would have remained a backwater as well, so Cardiff might still have been the ideal backwater capital for a backwater country (in the unlikely event of Wales requiring a capital at all under those circumstances). The rivers had cut their way through the South Wales plateau, thereby making the space for the railway and canal southward from the coalfields to the sea. They had deposited the mud to make a coastal plain on which a city could be built. The tidal range made the docking of ships suitable for an industrial age possible, when the iron industry and the coalfield needed the capacity to move bulk tonnages in and out of South Wales.

As a good Cardiffian, I always used to wonder why the Chartists of South Wales in 1839, assembling for their march on London to overturn the established order, agreed to meet in Newport and not Cardiff. How can you expect to mount a successful revolution if you start from Newport? It is all too easy for us to forget that in 1839 Newport was much more important than Cardiff. The people of Newport would have had as much right to look down on Cardiff as a one-horse town as happens all too frequently in reverse now.

Swansea and Merthyr in turn were much more important than Newport. So Cardiff was only number four in the hierarchy of industrial South Wales at the time when the Bute Docks were about to be developed. Those Docks were developed to satisfy the insatiable needs of importing iron ore to and exporting iron goods from Merthyr. The Glamorgan Canal was supplemented by the Taff Vale Railway and the 'green shoots' (and I mean real ones) were all in place for Cardiff's high-speed economic take-off. It was that take-off which in the end determined that it wasn't Swansea, Merthyr or Newport that became the capital of Wales.

Cardiff owes this debt, if it is a debt, to the iron deposits coinciding with the coal outcrop (and Mr Guest accidentally bumping into Mr Keen) on the mountainside at Dowlais above Merthyr. It also owes a debt to that doughty Bristolian, Isambard Kingdom Brunel. The replacement of the sailing-ship by the steam-powered vessel following the success of Brunel's *Great Eastern* was the key to the growth of coal exports from Cardiff, because its great innovation was to burn coal to raise steam. The South Wales Coalfield always was a devilishly difficult one to mine coal from—dangerous, gassy and dusty, heavily faulted, a great place to lose money, and a very occasional place to accumulate a fortune. Only born optimists sank mineshafts in South Wales.

High in price it may have been, but for firing ships' boilers, nothing could match South Wales dry steam coal. It could raise steam faster and burn cleaner with less ash and a higher power-to-weight ratio than any other known coal. The Royal Navy would burn nothing else and the Merchant Marine preferred it too. When pit after pit was being sunk in the Rhondda and the Cynon Valleys in the period after 1860, it was the ever-increasing number of steam ships' boilers that were waiting for the coal. That is why so many pits in South Wales were called Marine, Ocean, Maritime, Navigation or some other variant on the steamship theme. It was a primitive form of marketing, a century before you could do a B.A. Marketing degree at the University of Glamorgan in Treforest.

The steam-ship had about three-quarters of a century of domination between the decline of the sailing vessel and the rise of the oil-burning, slow-speed diesel. Wales and Cardiff grew phenomenally between 1850 and 1920. If Brunel was the unintending father of the explosive expansion of the coalfield, then Rudolf Diesel was the anti-hero, the inventor who equally unwittingly brought it all to an end.

To prove just how crucial that epoch was to Wales, consider what happened to Ireland over that same period—its population halved from 8 million to 4 million! Wales' population more than doubled from less than a million to more than 2.5 million.

Not forgetting the Potato Famine's devastating effects on Ireland, Wales was very much the exception in Europe in being able to find jobs locally for almost all its population. People emigrated from rural Wales of course, but they 'emigrated' in the main to industrial South Wales instead of to America. The contrast with Ireland is glaring because Ireland is right next-door and experienced the famine. Even if you think of prosperous countries like Germany, Sweden and Norway, they were sending millions of their 'surplus' agrarian population to North America, when Wales could accommodate most of it in the next county.

From being a backwater in 1830 Cardiff became by the 1880s the largest port in the world measured by crude tonnage of cargo handled. In some years it was New York, in other years Cardiff. The palm would swing back and fore across the Atlantic each year. Of course, there was no real comparison between the two ports. Cardiff dealt with one cargo, and one direction; New York dealt with hundreds, both import and export.

Cardiff was a monoculture, exporting coal from the Rhondda and the other dry-steam colliery areas to the bunkering stations used by the Royal and Merchant Navies in all parts of the world. Aden, Singapore, the Falklands, Cape Verde were all regular ports of call for the coal export boats stocking up the bunkers with the ships' favourite Four Star high-octane, unleaded fuel.

If there had been an OPEC for coal-producing countries in the late nineteenth century, Wales would have played a leading part in it (if there had been an independent Wales, that is). In fact, OPEC's headquarters would almost certainly have been in the Coal Exchange in Mountstuart Square, in the heart of the newly constructed business quarter adjoining the Pier Head.

This was the period when Cardiff hurtled past Newport, Swansea and Merthyr to become the biggest town in Wales. It also became a cosmopolitan city at the same time. Its growth not only drew in Welsh-speaking sea-captains, Cornish boiler-makers and thousands upon thousands of Irish navvies, it sucked in merchant seamen from all over the world. Newly recruited sailors and cabin-boys became a kind of return cargo of people as the coal-boats steamed home to Cardiff from the bunkering ports.

Should anyone want to know why we have a Somali community of several thousand today, the explanation is the Royal Navy coal-bunker station in Aden. The same is true for the Cape Verdians and the Chinese. Being 'cosmopolitan' sounds very smart these days; I am using the term literally to mean a lot of different people thrown together from all over the world. Cardiff in the late nineteenth century certainly bore no resemblance to late twentieth-century Knightsbridge or the King's Road in Chelsea. Being cosmopolitan meant that instead of just having anti-Irish Catholic and anti-black race-riots in Cardiff, we had anti-Chinese riots as well.

In a more indirect way, the reason why certain famous literary and artistic figures spent some of their formative years in Cardiff is really the same. The city was a magnet, the place where it was all happening; lots of money and jobs were available. That was why venturesome and talented young people such as Joseph Conrad, Eugene O'Neill and Henri Gaudier-Brezska came to Cardiff to work as shipping-clerks or seamen, for jobs or training. O'Neill has in his own way repaid his debt in his one-act play, *Bound East for Cardiff*. Come to think of it, I've never seen it performed in Cardiff.

Even more indirectly the explanation for the connection with Scott of the Antarctic is the same. The City Council did not have to advertize for high-profile but doomed causes to come to Cardiff. There was enough money floating about the Docks for Cardiff rather than London to be a perfectly logical launching-point for a major expedition, even one that was at the heart of Britain's imperial prestige.

Although Swansea and Newport were also expanding fast in that heroic period of Welsh economic development, Merthyr was not. Indeed, the gap between Cardiff and Merthyr became a yawning chasm after 1898. That was when the Guest Keen Iron and Steelworks were relocated from Merthyr to East Moors on Cardiff's docklands. For good if somewhat sentimental reasons the company kept the contact with Merthyr by naming the new complex the Dowlais Works after the hilltop village above Merthyr where the Guest Keen company, or if you prefer, the Industrial Revolution, was founded.

Even in the 1980s elsewhere in Britain, and right round the world, steelmakers argued over whether it was better to move steelworks to the coast, where you could unload high-quality foreign iron ores direct into the steelworks stockyard, or to leave the works where they were, with all their established skills and support services, and bring all the raw materials in. Do you bring Mohammet to the mountain, or in this case Merthyr, or do you take the mountain to Mohammet? Merthyr and Cardiff went through all that painful process to Merthyr's devastation and Cardiff's benefit before the turn of the century.

Cardiff suffered the devastation itself when 'The Dowlais' works closed in 1978, but in the intervening eighty years it gave the city the commercial diversification it needed to get away from being a coal-export port. What really makes Cardiff so different in character from Dublin or Edinburgh as a capital was the sheer size of its steel industry. Even as late as the mid-1960s over 11,000 worked in steel. Even in 1978 up to the last cast from the East Moors blast-furnaces (which I witnessed myself) 8,000 still had their employment in the industry.

The steel job-count is just over 2,000 now but the male pensioner population of Cardiff sometimes seems to me to consist almost entirely of people who once worked either in the Dowlais or in the GKN re-rolling mills. What is more, almost every young man from Cardiff who ever went to university worked his long vacations at the steelworks during the summer shut-down, hundreds of them every year absorbing the hot-metal culture in their formative years.

That is not to say Dublin and Edinburgh don't have any big industries. It's more really a question of balance—between the lawyers and administrators on the one hand, who find employment from the 'wordsmith and pen-pushing' capital city, and those on the other, who work in occupations which could be on the other side of the moon from the world of the national bureaucracy.


## DOWLAIS OR DALLAS?

Cardiff's personality as a city is still much more affected by the steel industry than Dublin is by the Guinness Brewery or Jacobs Biscuits, or Edinburgh by the William Younger Brewery or Peebles Switchgear. A steelworks could be located anywhere, after all. Guest Keen never actually gained any benefit from being in a capital city. It might indeed have lost out from it, because decision-makers at the top level of government could and often did conclude that it detracted from the tone of the capital to have a big smokestack industry in town. It put a bit of grit into the atmosphere both literally and metaphorically.

When I was a young civil servant in the Welsh Office in the mid-1960s, working on Wales' very own Five Year Plan, I was gob-smacked by the hostility of top civil servants to the existence of a large-scale steel industry in Cardiff. 'Let's get rid of it', they said to my absolute horror. 'Then Cardiff can concentrate on the service industries and become a real capital city'.

The view from Cathays Park and the suburbs to the north where these mandarins lived was very different from the view from Splott. I should add that the mandarins were wrong on this issue as on so many others. It is little wonder that they are known as satsumas in Whitehall, because the Welsh Office is not reckoned to be a fully-fledged 'proper' Government Department.

The hot-metal sub-culture of Splott, Tremorfa, Adamsdown and Llanrumney always has been pretty well sealed off from the imperial administration sub-culture of Cathays Park. Would the satsumas ever have understood how steelworkers were served at the Grosvenor pub in Splott Road, just yards from the works' entrance? When the 10 p.m. shift finished they had only half an hour's drinking-time left. The landlord used to allow the regulars to throw their two-shilling pieces into a bucket filled with water, because a till or bar-staff could not keep up with that kind of raging collective thirst.

I recall being in a Cardiff pub with an adult student who had been to Ruskin College, Oxford, before getting into Cardiff University. He mentioned to another drinker that before becoming a student he'd worked ten years on the blast furnaces in Rotherham. In pubs in Oxford, that line had evidently been a show-stopper. This other guy simply responded, cool as a cucumber, 'Oh yeah, was that back-end or front-end?'

The strength of the Cardiff accent is a tribute to the strength of that industrial sub-culture. This uneasy co-existence—the tension between the two cultures in the city—is what gives Cardiff its special character. The creative tension is not what a stray visitor from the planet Mars or Workingham might expect to find. It's not between the non-Welsh-speaking and the Welsh-speaking but between the industrial and the satsuma way of life.

Much as the English are quite convinced that Cardiff has at least half-a-dozen coal-mines, when it has none, the professional classes would prefer to imagine that Cardiff has no steelworks when it actually does. Now and again the existence of the steel sub-culture would impinge on the public life of the city—Harry Hitchings' high altitude sit-in on the top of the steelworks water-tower was one example, because it was such an innovation in strike tactics. Three men sacked for watching blue film-shows organized during the nightshift was another. The dodgy air-quality figures for Cardiff was always another cause of tut-tutting in Rhiwbina and Cyncoed, but it was definitely a part of Cardiff's life. You could avoid it only by never going south of Newport Road. The city at large was forced to make its mind up about whether it wanted a steel industry or not on Boxing Day 1973, when the British Steel Corporation announced its intention of closing the East Moors works. That was the time when the citizens of Cardiff had to decide whether the steel industry was a nuisance-factor in a nice modern capital city, or else the foundation stone of the local economy.

I don't say the *Western Mail* is a perfect barometer of public opinion, but the tortuous process by which the editorial line changed bit by bit from supporting the closure to supporting the steelworkers showed the dilemma. Even in the steelworks itself the campaign had a bad start. It was likewise in the level of public sympathy out in the community. When it finally got going, it was a remarkably effective one. The struggle went on from 1973 until 1978. It finished with the new steelworks being built in Tremorfa, although it provided jobs for only 300 or so compared with 4,600 at East Moors. It was built by GKN and not British Steel (but British Steel had to take a half-share in it five years later).

Not only did the workers' 'Save our Steelworks' campaign get the backing of the City Council and the County Council, it had the backing of the Man and Woman on the Gabalfa omnibus. At first sight it might be thought that shouldn't be a surprise, that local patriotism should ensure it anyway. But most steel-making areas were different from Cardiff. They were usually more like Port Talbot or Ebbw Vale or Shotton, where the steelworks was the only show in town. In Cardiff that public support had to be worked for and kept up with frequent liberal applications of campaign fertilizer. Cardiff did unite behind the workforce, and got a much better understanding afterwards of where industry fitted into the life and image of the city.

This ambivalence about where the steel industry fitted into its economy even extends to where it fits into the city's cultural landscape. Probably the best paintings of Cardiff ever done are Lionel Walden's stunning canvases of the docks and steelworks in the late 1920s and Graham Sutherland's efforts inside East Moors when he was an official War Artist during the Second World War. Can you see them on display in Cardiff? Only with enormous difficulty.

In the Musée d'Orsay in Paris you can see Walden's 'Les Docks à Cardiff' proudly and prominently displayed both on the wall and in the museum's catalogue. In the National Museum of Wales in Cathays Park, which after all incorporates the Municipal Art Gallery of Cardiff, there is a miniature version of the same view about four inches square hanging inside the gallery but tucked in on the return wall next to the doorway. Its proper sister full-size painting hangs precariously at the top of the stairs outside the gallery. You would require a double-jointed giraffe's neck to see it. It doesn't fit in to the idea of 'chocolate box' rural Wales landscape painting, so it is hung in shame above the tradesmen's entrance, as it were.

To see Sutherland's wartime studies of East Moors it is even worse. You have to go to the Graham Sutherland Gallery in Picton Castle just outside Haverfordwest, a hundred miles west of the subject of the paintings. Others lie in the storage vaults of the Imperial War Museum. Not only are they not on permanent display, they have never been on temporary loan in the city either. If the National Museum would like to see more steelworkers from Splott and their families visiting the Museum, then why do they go to such lengths to avoid hanging paintings of the steelworks in the galleries? It's not as if there were a lot of scenes of other aspects of life and landscape around Cardiff to choose from.

Until about 1980, the dockers, both wet and dry, and the steelworkers made up a major part of the city's lifestyle, especially south of Newport Road and Cowbridge Road, Cardiff's equivalent of the Mason-Dixon Line. Thousands went to work for Curran's who made everything from saucepans to Sherman Tanks. There the only questions you were asked if you applied for a job, were 'Are you a Roman Catholic?' and 'Are you a member of a trade union?' Provided the first answer was Yes and the second No, you were in. This background in turn gave rise to the Cardiff definition of loneliness being a Protestant working for Curran's. What went on south of the old A48 proceeded with very little contact with the later and better-off suburbs to the north of the city centre.

Between 1966 and 1968 the second largest strike in British industrial history took place among the boilermakers employed in one of the dry docks in Cardiff. Its two years duration is only exceeded by the Bethesda slate quarrymen's three-year effort in 1901-4. Did it have any impact in Rhiwbina? The Sherman girls (the pools coupon-checkers) and the Freeman girls (the cigar-rollers) contributed to Cardiff's employment and social culture in much the same way amongst women.

Much of the heavy industrial base and the big concentrations of employment in traditional industries and offices is now shrunk or gone. By 1990, when Associated British Ports sacked all the dockers (yes, all the dockers in the Port of Cardiff), there was barely a peep out of anyone, so much had the balance of power changed within the city.


THE PEN-PUSHERS' PARADISE

What do people in Cardiff do for a living now, now that steel is shrunk, the Ely paper-mill has lost its last paper-making machine, and Powell Duffryn has closed its Maindy railway-waggon works after a hundred years? Ship-repairing used to employ 2,000 until the strike in 1968—now it's 200. One thing is for sure, the old skills are not going to come back. We use our cities for different purposes now. The muscle-work has gone, much of the craft has gone. What instead? The coal export trade is certainly not coming back. In fact, Cardiff Docks are now partly dependent on the coal import trade, staggering though that may seem to the historically-minded.

The search for a new economic base has been going on for a long time now. Public administration in the form of the Welsh Office and the Inland Revenue, plus the two County Councils, all provide stability in the city's economic life, just as in any other capital city. The problem has been in providing the choice of jobs. Not everybody is cut out for pushing a pen. What about those who want to work in the private sector—where will they work? Will those who want to work in offices be working where they can make real decisions or will they be in somebody else's 'back office'?

What about those who don't want to push a pen or tap a keyboard for a living? You can build a *Canberra* or an *Ottawa* straight off the drawing-board with no problem, if you've got the money. But can you convert a port and steelworks city like Cardiff into an industry-free zone? Those older occupations and industries and the way of life that went with them have, after all, been around for a century-and-a-half.

The Welsh Office was founded in 1964 as an independent Department of State, although small devolved offices of the London Ministries of Health and Housing were set up in Cathays Park, the civic centre of Cardiff, in the 1920s. These bits and pieces of administrative powers delegated to Wales were largely due to the influence of Tom Jones of Rhymney, Cabinet Secretary between the wars.

The Inland Revenue was moved out of London during the Second World War to escape the Blitz. The tax affairs of all civil servants, all pensioners, all MPs, VIPs, the Secret Service and the armed forces and the minor royals have all been dealt with in Llanishen in the northern suburbs of Cardiff since the beginning of the war. Between 1974 and 1979 a really determined effort was made to disperse Civil Service jobs out of London. The Export Credit Guarantees Department and Companies House trundled down the M4, each providing a thousand or so jobs.

In the world of private finance, there was a brief period from about 1958 to 1968 when local finance expert Julian Hodge had a dream of creating a banking centre to challenge the financial deal-making power of at least Edinburgh, if not the City of London as well. For a while the somnolent Cardiff Stock Exchange, where there was always time for another yarn about the good old days of the coal trade, woke up. Cardiff did build up a lot of expertise in the down-market end of the financial services market, hire-purchase and other ways of providing finance and 'banking for the unbanked'. Charlotte Square in Edinburgh and the City of London were about as interested in the unbanked as they were in the unwashed. The dream never got off the ground. The H.P. company was sold to the Standard and Chartered Bank. The other pillars of the Hodge Empire were mostly sold as well. Local control was lost. Julian Hodge didn't give up the dream though, and had another go at it fifteen years ago by founding the Bank of Wales. The ambition this time was to provide development funds for expanding Welsh industry.

The problem was that expanding Welsh businesses don't suddenly up sticks and leave their previous banks for a new one just because the new bank's headquarters are in Wales. Businesses don't switch banks to take part in an economic experiment. It might be different in America or Asia but in Europe it takes many decades, if not centuries, to build up a bank of any susbstance. The Bank of Wales got as far as starting on building new headquarters in Kingsway. By the time the building was finished, the recession of the late 1980s had knocked the Big Idea off course once again.

The Bank of Scotland took over the Bank of Wales. Edinburgh had to bail the struggling Cardiff bank out at the price of the bank's independence. Julian Hodge is now pursuing the dream yet again with the Carlisle Bank—his third Cardiff-based regional bank. This time, however, it is being developed with less overtly expressed ambitions about building up a major financial centre.

There was a lesson here—that one person's efforts can't diversify a city on their own. If there ever was any hope of developing a financial services industry in Cardiff, then it wouldn't work just as Hodge City. If it ever was going to succeed then a whole financial community was needed, raising capital, refloating companies in trouble, syndicating loans—not just one group of largely interdependent financial companies. It's the monoculture of the coal-export trade all over again. Never depend on just one industry, one business or one big financier, however rich or ambitious. One swallow does not a summer make. One cargo does not a port make. One bank does not a financial centre make.

Maybe the whole idea was misconceived. Perhaps a city of less than 300,000 people serving an industrial region of less than 2 million could never be a significant centre for the financial services industries anyway. That base may be too small, even for a wealthy area of two million people. Since South Wales was hardly a by-word for wealth, prosperity and capital accumulation, it just wasn't on. Building a diverse and sound economic future is a painstaking and never-ending job, a bit like painting the Forth Bridge. Cardiff has always looked for what will never be there—the one Big Hit that will make all the difference between poverty and prosperity, obscurity and prominence. But there is no Holy Grail of Mammon out there waiting for us to find it, which will provide that permanent guarantee of wealth.

The other mirage pretending to be a bright new economic future for the city that pops up from time to time is speculative property development. Every time there is a property boom in Britain, some seer will confidently proclaim that a new Golden Age is dawning for Cardiff which is comparable to that of 1870-1914.

During the 1972-3 office-building boom, I can recall an Anglo-Welsh commercial estate agent breezing in from London, spending some hours looking around the city, then pronouncing himself delighted with the potential he could observe. He announced grandly that with the right planning permission for tower office blocks and so forth, he could confidently forecast that Cardiff could 'become another Croydon'! Wawee! Really? Gee, thanks. He also claimed he liked the Pearl Building.

Maybe though in one sense, another Croydon is what we have become on the quiet. The big success in getting new jobs has been in insurance and finance back office jobs. Because Cardiff is part of the M4 Corridor, some finance companies have forgotten to stop off at Swindon or Bristol. They have travelled on across the Severn Bridge to Cardiff—the AA Insurance subsidiary in 1977, the Chemical Bank of New York in 1983, the National Provident Institution in 1987. More than one swallow, but not exactly a summer.

The only problem with these dispersals from the south-east of England, whether in the Civil Service or the private sector, is that they don't give us 'critical mass' in financial services, because there is not enough decision-making-type employment being dispersed. Beggars can't be choosers, of course. At the moment, all that takes place in those tower-blocks is the processing of claims and mortgages. We need to persuade some of the companies dispersed here to bring down the real McCoy as well—the decisions over what they invest their funds in.

There isn't any longer a Cardiff Stock Exchange worthy of the name. We know now that it has proved next to impossible to build up local banking. There is therefore no medium for recycling the savings of the people of Wales into businesses in Wales needing funds to expand. It's been tried and so far at least it hasn't come off. We are too small, our original expertise in coal-trading isn't worth a light in the 1990s. Steel—our other area of expertise—isn't a growth industry. The other new industries are ones where we only have the branch factories in Wales. The decision-makers are across the Severn Bridge or halfway around the world in Japan or Taiwan. Branch factories don't need locally-owned banks and expensive office space in skyscrapers in Cardiff to house the company's headquarters.

This has a fundamental effect on the present and future shape of downtown Cardiff. In the state capitals of America, Australia, Spain or Germany, the main business district will be dominated by the skyscraper office blocks occupied by the H.Q.s of the locally-owned banks and insurance companies. If we are not likely to have any locally-owned banks, we are not going to have

37

that familiar capital city skyline of tower office blocks in our Financial Quarter, which we see when we watch *Dallas* or *Dynasty*.

That is why we need to be wary of estate agents and property developers promising a new Golden Age for Cardiff. We don't need any more pipe-dreams, 20:20 Euro-visions and mission statements. We need realism about where we stand and where we are capable of going. I've seen more artists' impressions and estate agents' brochures of the glamorous skyscraper future of the centre of Cardiff looking like JR's Dallas or Alexis Carrington's Denver, than I've had hot dinners. Public relations hype gets you nowhere in the real world.

If any property wallah was mad enough to build us a glittering new skyscraper office block complex in Cardiff because he had a vision of Cardiff as Croydon West, it would remain a white elephant for decades. Only a Government Department would be able to afford the rent. If we are not going to be able to develop a Financial Quarter, then Cardiff is going to need to look elsewhere for employment.


SQUARE PEGS IN A ROUND MELTING POT?

When I got back to Cardiff from spending two years in America thirty years ago, I half-expected that it would be a nice quiet down-home type of experience. I found a big row going on that was straight out of *On the Waterfront*. It was over a Cardiff-Irish foreman who had been taking kickbacks from Yemeni new arrivals for helping them get jobs at an engineering factory on the Docks. The new arrivals from the Middle East would go straight off the boat to see the sheikh. He would give them a letter of introduction to the foreman. He in turn would fix them up with a job on the lowly-paid radiator production-line, in return for 10% or so of their wages.

One young Yemeni who could not abide this corrupting of his fellow-countrymen, and did not mind disturbing the established order of things, wanted help from us lefty political types. We used to meet in the Alexandra Hotel (known to one and all as the Alex) on the corner of Queen Street next to the railway station of the same name. The young Yemeni did succeed in busting the system. It ended in the trial and conviction of the foreman. That kind of thing probably couldn't happen now, for the primary reason that there are not enough factories around, and that particular one closed not long ago.

I never went in too much for the official line from City Hall that Cardiff was a beautifully harmonious mixture of many peoples—the Irish and the West Country people who had come for the heavy work of buildings and working the docks, the Spaniards who had come over on the iron-ore boats to work in Guest Keen's blast-furnaces, the seamen from West Africa and the Horn of Africa and the world over to make Tiger Bay worthy of a film, the Jews who had been pushed out of Eastern Europe by pogroms in Poland and Russia, and even the occasional Welsh woollyback as well. I just didn't buy it. How could I?

It was certainly a heady mixture of peoples. Anyone can see that from the names of the four most famous literary figures to emerge from Cardiff—Roald Dahl, R. S. Thomas, Bernice Rubens and Dannie Abse. How odd, you might think, for three of the best writers produced by the capital of Wales to be Norwegian and Jewish by background. If you were from Cardiff you would find nothing odd about it at all. Indeed, the odd one out is undoubtedly R. S. Thomas, the one with ·the Welsh surname, even probably in his own eyes. The outstanding sporting figures tell the same ethnic story—Peerless Jim Driscoll and Paolo Radmilovic, one Irish and one Polish, are the only Cardiff sporting stars to have been selected for the World Sports Hall of Fame, for boxing and swimming respectively.

The pertinent question was whether this more typically American than British admixture of peoples was harmoniously blending or not. The evidence from the historical record was not favourable. Cardiff has had anti-Catholic race-riots, anti-black race-riots and unusually for British society, in 1911 we even had anti-Chinese race-riots. That happened as part of the nation-wide recognition strike by the National Union of Seamen against the

Shipping Federation, 'Captain' Edward Tupper 'VC' (he wasn't a captain or a VC) was sent down to the city by the NUS (the seamen's variety, not the students') to foment trouble. He and the local seamen's strike committee burnt down the Chinese laundries and the lodging-houses used by Chinese seamen. Indeed, about the only kind of racial trouble Cardiff's history books have no record of, was riots between the Welsh and the English!

I also recall in the early 1960s a dispute in the dry-docks between black and white ship-repairers, all based on what kind of union card each group of dockers carried. The men were all in the same union, but some were 'registered' and had first rights to a job. Others, mainly black, were casuals, but were by custom and practice always allowed to finish a ship-repair contract once they had started it. In this case, the registered men wanted to evict the casuals before they'd finished the job on a particular ship. Physical violence was being threatened from both sides.

If this was a melting-pot, then it was evident to me that someone had turned the heat off before melting temperature had been reached. Maybe all melting-pots are like this. They don't melt, they just get stirred a bit. It certainly gave me an insight into life in the raw that I had never got from my youthful forays into Cardiff on Saturday mornings on the 33 bus from Radyr, or even on the annual tram-ride to the Pier Head to catch the White Funnel steamer over to Weston-super-Mare. When I was fifteen I thought the most exciting thing about Cardiff was having a cup of coffee, mostly froth, in the Kardomah Café! When I was twenty-five I thought there weren't enough hours in the day to cram in all the excitement the city could provide.

I actually believed, perhaps I still do, that Cardiff had mastered 90% of the trick of having the intimate feel of a small town, a collection of village communities, combined with most of the cosmopolitan attractions of a big city like London or New York. When I returned it still only had two book shops and two sports-goods shops, but it had the politics, the food and the music that I was looking for. I much preferred jazz and folk to classical or pop music. Above all I preferred my music live. Nothing could be better than to go from a political meeting in the back-room of the Old Arcade pub into the lounge bar and there would be the Hennessys rehearsing. This was before BBC Wales regrettably turned them into Yr Hennessys. Well, I mean to say, it should have been Yr Hennessyau, shouldn't it? I was so jealous of the Hennessys' musical talent that I wanted to form a folk-group as well. I was going to call it Flatholm Lighthouse and the Foghorns, because with a name like that I thought it wouldn't matter that we couldn't sing.

Indeed, it is one of my major claims to being an ordinary citizen of Cardiff that I have never been to a performance by the Welsh National Opera Company. But I don't half miss the Quebec. This was the mecca of casual followers of jazz. It was the tattiest pub imaginable—it never had concerts that you bought tickets for. It barely had toilets. You just bought your pint and listened to the music. Visitors to Cardiff could never believe the quality of the performers and all for free whether they came to the jazz in the evenings or the Opportunity Knocks variety show that would spontaneously combust at Sunday lunchtimes.

The brewery closed the pub twenty years ago and 'it'—the musical mecca that went with it—didn't move to any other pub; it just died. I think the opening of the Four Bars Jazz pub, opposite the Castle, was Brain's Brewery's penance for having a bad conscience over the killing of the Quebec. Like the Radyr Locos, the Quebec never came back.

What about the food? What most Cardiffians, maybe most people want when eating out is to eat well without being pretentious. It all depends: how unpretentious can you get? One friend of mine was ordering a meal with his Dad in the Louis. Lil and May, now into their sixth decade as waitresses at the Louis, pointed out a large group across the restaurant happily tucking into their steaks. 'That's the Nolan Sisters', said one proudly. 'And they're no trouble', chimed in the other.

I believe there is one pub-cum-steakhouse on the edge of town which offers, or at least used to offer, the 'Cardiff Challenge'— steaks so big that if you could finish with a clean plate, you didn't have to pay. Not long after the offer started, a rival establishment started serving what were claimed to be even bigger steaks on the same terms. This was advertised as the Universal Challenge. Moving directly from having the biggest steaks in Cardiff to the biggest in the universe shows confidence. Perhaps too much confidence, since I don't think either steakhouse does this Clean Plate—No Pay deal now. We are back to our normal modesty about anything fancy in the cooking line.

A property developer acquaintance of mine took his wife to Veeraswamy's, the Indian restaurant to end all Indian restaurants in Mayfair, to celebrate their silver wedding a little while ago. After ordering their main courses, they were asked what they wanted 'to go with it'. My acquaintance half-facetiously wondered out loud to his wife what the reaction would be if they were to ask for 'half-and-half' (half rice-half chips, Cardiff's only known contribution to gastronomic history). The waiter burst out with unconstrained delight, 'Oh, so you are from Cardiff too!' and was overjoyed to explain that he used to live in Grangetown!

Those early Indian restaurants were a big factor in breaking down social distinctions in Cardiff. Before curry-houses, the middle-classes went to restaurants and the working-classes to cafés or chip-shops, or ate at home. But everybody ate in Indian restaurants. Now that the Welsh Folk Museum at St. Fagans has discovered the twentieth century, perhaps an early Cardiff Indian restaurant is the logical next step. They have finally progressed beyond their rural obsession to exhibits like the row of Merthyr workers' cottages. They have rebuilt a typical Workmen's Institute from the Valleys and Lord David Owen's grandpa's Ogmore Vale grocery store. I can't see why by the turn of the century they couldn't re-create the old Lights of Asia and the aromatic and highly-flavoured atmosphere of 1960s Bridge Street after dark.

After all, if rural Wales is part of Wales and the Valleys are part of Wales, the extraordinary logical ultimate conclusion is surely that Cardiff must be part of Wales as well. Well, maybe that would be going too far for the Welsh Folk Museum.

Until Jim Callaghan became Prime Minister and George Thomas Mr Speaker, Cardiff's best-known had been Jimmy Thomas, a railway trade union leader from Splott and Colonial Secretary in the early Labour Government in 1929-1931. He gave an official dinner at which the Chinese Ambassador to the Court of St James' was the guest of honour. Jimmy's knowledge of China and the Chinese was limited to childhood study of the pages of *Comic Cuts*. Making light conversation with the Ambassador over the first course, all Jimmy offered by way of small talk was 'You likee soupee?'. After the Ambassador had later spoken in faultless English for forty minutes and sat down, he turned to Thomas and said, 'You likee speechee?' It's too good a story for us to worry too much about its total accuracy.

If Jimmy Thomas was a representative of Cardiff's working population then maybe we are still looking for the true spirit of the middle-class. It must be there but where is its stamp? If there was a real-life Miss Jean Brodie who helped mould the mind and speech of Morningside to give the Edinburgh bourgeoisie its special house-style, she or he was mighty successful. I suppose the nearest equivalent to Jean Brodie in Cardiff was Cliff Diamond, the seemingly permanent headmaster of post-war Cardiff High School for Boys.

The city always has been divided between those who speak with the proper Kairdiff accent and those who don't. Cliff Diamond took it upon himself to rid his flock of the dreaded accent before they left the High School, as though it were a social disease. I dare say other headteachers of the city's Grammar Schools tried to do the same in a less single-minded way. They just weren't there for the many decades that Diamond was, to exert the same kind of cultural influence.

One of his favourite ways of shaming Kairdiff-talking young lads from Splott or Adamsdown who had passed the 11 Plus high enough up the city's scholastic lists to be admitted to his academy, was to ask them to recite the words 'Hark, Hark, the Lark' out loud. If they failed this linguistic litmus test, he would tell them (in front of hundreds of other boys), 'Good God, boy! If you go on speaking like that, you'll finish up as a Cardiff City Councillor!' How these youngsters made out on Splott Road after being linguistically reprogrammed and brainwashed in this way is hard to imagine.

The key difference between Cardiff and Edinburgh, however, is that the accent of the Edinburgh bourgeoisie is both distinctly Scottish and regarded as fully the equal in social snob-status to the Oxbridge English accent. You can't say that about the Cardiff professional classes and their accent. It is neither different enough from Oxbridge nor is it accepted as being OK for BBC Radio 4 announcers. It is not only Edinburgh whose bourgeois accent is accepted as being totally different from Oxbridge but equal to it. Dublin has achieved this exalted status as well. When you hear the nicely modulated tones of Dr Anthony Clare or Frank Delaney on Radio 4, you realize that middle-class Cardiff has got a long way to go to obtain equal recognition.

The best-known member of the British Establishment who has sprung from the Cardiff professional classes is possibly Lord Walter Marshall, ex-boss of Britain's electricity industry and Margaret Thatcher's favourite scientist. His colleagues thought he talked a bit funny. Anybody from Cardiff can recognize his accent straight away. His colleagues in Harwell and Whitehall couldn't. When they were asked to guess where he was from, they would hazard a guess at something East European— 'Hungarian? Lithuanian?' Maybe Cliff Diamond should have given as much thought to what he was programming into the speech patterns of his young charges, as he did to de-programming them from saying the dread, 'Airk, Airk, the Lairk in Kairdiff Airms Pairk'.

Diamond's dire prediction about talking like a councillor was not a party political one. Both Tory and Labour City Councillors did speak proper-Kairdiff then. I can recall Alderman Frank Chapman, the Lord Mayor in 1956, introducing the ultra-Brahmin Mrs Pandit, India's Ambassador to the UN and sister of Nehru, the Prime Minister, to a packed-out meeting in the cavernous Wood St. Congregational Chapel. Looking at the serried thousands who had assembled, he said, 'There must be arfaKairdiff here tonight'. If Cliff Diamond was present, I am sure he would have been thinking, 'Why can't the Lord Mayor of Cardiff speak the King's English as well as India's Ambassador to the United Nations?' Because the Lord Mayor wasn't a Brahmin was perhaps the answer.

The local working-class accent—the same accent as is found in Barry, Newport and the eastern half of Penarth—is quite distinct. But outside South Wales, it suffers from the same lack of recognition as a genuine regional accent, as its middle-class opposite number. It's not used by working-class music-hall comics, the way the Welsh Valleys, Merseyside, Lancashire and Glasgow accents have been (though Stan Stennet is an honourable exception). It is still abhorred by BBC Wales radio announcers and disc-jockeys with the one exception of Frank Hennessy.

The Valleys accent certainly is recognized outside Wales. Glasgow and Liverpool's accents are recognized, too. Why isn't Cardiff's? It's that old lack of self-confidence again, which arises from being a city that is too small ever to be a metropolis. Perhaps it's because Cardiffians are so conscious of the accent divide in their own city, it leaves them too exhausted to establish acceptance of either style of speech outside the city.

Some people say that blue-collar Kairdiff is hard listening for those who suffer from Aesthete's Ear. It is, they say, invariably adenoidal, even when the speaker doesn't have a cold. Maybe it's the rain or the dust from the steelworks that did it. Its defining characteristics involve the distinctive long 'a' turned into an 'air'. Then there is the interrogative lift at the end of all sentences which turns every statement into a question, plus like the insertion like of the word 'like' between like every other word like.

Because it is not among the list of dialects well registered amongst the authentic 'regional' accents around Hampstead dinner-tables, the film *Tiger Bay* did not bother to find a single actor using the accent. This was in a film trying hard to be an authentic slice of specifically Cardiff low-life. Very disconcerting that film was for all of us locals. We saw the cargo-boat bringing

45

Horst Buchholz into port at the start of the film dipping under Newport Transporter Bridge. Then, after docking, Buchholz jumps off the ship straight into Loudoun Square in the heart of Tiger Bay and everyone is speaking with a Rhondda Valley accent! Using actors who spoke with a Cardiff accent would not have sounded authentic, would it?

Cinema audiences around the English-speaking world would be able to 'place' the film in South Wales, when they heard the Valleys accent. They would be baffled by hearing the Cardiff accent. So the authentic local accent goes out of the window. Of course the name Tiger Bay places the location in Cardiff Docks in the same way as a Valleys accent. It's just that the accent and the location don't go together, except that is, to English film-makers. Everybody has heard of Tiger Bay and everyone can recognize a Valleys accent. It would be nice to have the chance in some future film to make the point that Tiger Bay and the Valleys accent do not properly fit together, but Tiger Bay and 'Airk Airk the Lairk' do.

However, the British film industry has itself disappeared like old Loudoun Square, the Radyr Locos and the Quebec, so this is now an academic point, but a sore one. After all, Nottingham is no bigger than Cardiff, but all the actors in *Saturday Night and Sunday Morning* used Nottingham accents. That tells you how insignificant Cardiff's place is in the social and cultural scheme of things.

It is probably no more than an unconsidered oddity, but the number-one hallmark of the blue-collar Kairdiff accent, the 'Airk Airk the Lairk' vowel-sound, is pretty much the same in the South Glamorgan dialect of Welsh as well. I find that ironic because the conventional wisdom is that there has always been enmity between Welsh-speakers and the city's working-classes who talk proper Kairdiff. Would that divide be there, if there was more awareness that both groups were united across a language-barrier by having the same way of distorting the long 'a'?

The financial and official support for the teaching of Welsh and English and Welsh bilingual road-signs engender some resentment. Not a lot, but it can be given a nudge, sometimes with point, sometimes with humour by populist journalists. You know the kind of thing, 'If they're going to have a Welsh Language Society, we are going to set up a Kairdiff Langwidge Sitey'. Actually it was me who won the Drama Gold Medal at the first Kairdiff Langwidge Sitey Eisteddfod. We were asked to imagine that Ivor Novello had bumped into Joseph Conrad and Eugene O'Neill in a Cardiff pub in the early years of this century, and to write the dialogue for the ensuing conversation. My winning entry was very short. It was 'Three pints of Dark, please'. Mind you, you mustn't believe everything you read in books.

The KLS does exist in a kind of a way and it did mount some sort of campaign against the closures of the Wimborne pub and the Bomb and Dagger Social Club in Portmanmoor Road in Splott next to where the steelworks once stood. They claimed the capital city of Wales was in danger of losing some of the finer points of the Splott sub-dialect of true Kairdiffese. They claimed the club was the *locus classicus* of the Kairdiff accent.

The KLS campaign to save the club from closure on cultural grounds was just a bit of fun. On another level, it was a protest against the lack of acceptance of the Cardiff accent anywhere outside the city. It was a plea for the next authentic 'slice of life in downtown Cardiff' TV series, play or one day maybe a second Tiger Bay film, to use the proper accent. Can you for a minute imagine the films made of Roddy Doyle's 'slice of life on a Dublin council estate' books, *The Commitments,* being made with Belfast-accented actors? *Bread* would be dead and *Brookside* all dried up without Liverpool accents; that is what gives them their essential local flavour. No one writer, not even Andrew Davies, has yet done that for Cardiff. The KLS type of sensitivity is not wholly without foundation.

That other sensitivity among the mass of citizens against too much of a fuss being made of preserving the Welsh language is not manifested against the Welsh-speakers who speak the local South Glamorgan Welsh. They never get jobs with the BBC anyway. The number of people who can still speak that dialect within the city boundaries is probably no more than half-a-dozen now. You can hardly harbour resentment against half-a-dozen, can you? I can just about recall a lady who spoke genuine Whitchurch dialect Welsh, when I attended the Tabernacl Baptist Sunday School in the Hayes in the 1950s.

Further north there are perhaps a hundred or so more in the surrounding hilltop villages of Gwaelod-y-Garth and Pentyrch in Mid Glamorgan. They are all now well into pensionable age. It is quite possible that before the year 2000 there will be no one left who can speak genuine Cardiff Welsh. That dialect will have gone for ever. Should the event be marked in some way? Is it a matter of concern for Cardiff, as the capital of Wales, that its own local Welsh dialect will probably no longer exist by the turn of the century?

The survival of the language in the authentic local dialect until now is little short of a social miracle. The triangle of villages around the Garth mountain are only six to eight miles from City Hall. Their sheep-farms and quarries and their isolation from the main transport routes have enabled that strange survival to occur, while places much further west and north of Cardiff lost the language decades ago. Maybe all the dialects of Welsh will die out not long after the turn of the millennium. Shortly thereafter Welsh will become the first language in the world to be spoken entirely by university graduates.

There will of course be any number of people in Cardiff speaking Welsh in the year 2000, either because they are attending Welsh-medium schools, or used to, or because they have moved to the city from Tregaron or Blaenau Ffestiniog for jobs in the BBC or the Welsh Office. That is where the ill-feeling can arise. There is some resentment undoubtedly felt by people in downtown Cardiff concerning official support for the Welsh language. Sometimes it's just there. Sometimes it's generated by skilled populist newspaper columnists like Dan O'Neill, and given the form of contemporary folk-song in Frank Hennessy's 'I'm an ardinairy citizen o' Kairdiff'.

It may only be seven miles from Tiger Bay on the waterfront up to Morganstown at the northern city-limits but it's a long way socially and linguistically. Both communities have more experience of adversity than of prosperity. That therefore cannot be where the resentment comes from against too much Welsh. It's more a kind of bewilderment, I think, at the decline of the old skills and jobs in the steelworks and ship-repair yards, and the rise of new jobs in the media and public adminstration. Those displaced from the old jobs lost on the Docks simply do not have the paper qualifications to fill the new jobs. 'How am I supposed to get a job at the Folk Museum/BBC/S4C, when I don't speak Welsh?' The capital city functions of Cardiff have been imposed quite suddenly in this century on an industrial and dockland base, and this transformation is bound to produce casualties.

Unlike Dublin and Edinburgh, those capital city functions have not had centuries to bed down in the life of the city and then to grow organically. That's why there is tension between those who are qualified and those who are not. The need to speak Welsh is seen as just one more of the qualifications required for the new jobs in the new bureaucracies. Fluency in Welsh stands as a surrogate for all the other difficult qualifications as well, like university degree, business-studies certificates, five years of management experience, personnel diplomas, and so on.


## POLITICS

In the spring of 1964, we organized what I think was the first anti-apartheid demonstration in Wales against a visiting South African colour-bar sports team. It was only the Bowls Team, but you have to start somewhere. It was all done from the lounge of the Alexandra Hotel, where students rubbed shoulders socially with dockers and railwaymen, all mixing freely, sometimes easily sometimes not. The route was arranged with the constabulary. We had to march up the full length of Queen Street past the Castle, across Canton Bridge and turn right into Sophia Gardens where the Bowls International was to be played. Political demonstrations were, or so I was told, not all that common in Cardiff. The normal way of letting off political steam was by way of a packed meeting in the Cory Hall next door to the Alex.

When we agreed the route for the march we could see why marches were not exactly the 'in thing' in Cardiff. It's hard to credit now, but Queen Street then was not only the busiest shopping street in Wales, it was also the busiest stretch of highway as well. All those 20-ton steel lorries carrying steel coils from Port Talbot to London and the Midlands used to inch their way along Queen Street practically brushing the carrier-bags of the shoppers. Most of Cardiff's suburban buses also had stops on Queen Street. The pedestrian crush on the pavement outside the stretch from Marks and Spencer to Boots passing Woolworth on the way was unimaginable.

We had one policeman front and back, but we were definitely taking our life in our hands. The space for our march was in a three-foot-wide channel between the pavement and the steel lorries and buses. Where the pedestrian traffic was at its densest it always spilled onto the road anyway, so we definitely got to know intimately all the engineering design details of the side and rear of BRS 20-ton flat-back steel-coil-carrying lorries that day. If you could organize a successful march in circumstances like that, you could organize a march anywhere. South Africa was an international issue, but it did have particular resonance for us for reasons of rugby and race relations. To be honest, we still don't know if the outstanding black rugby-players from the Docks and Ely, Billy Boston, Colin Dixon, Clive Sullivan and Frank Wilson, would have been selected for Wales, if they had not 'gone North' to play professional Rugby League.

By the time marching against apartheid-related Springbok teams was a normal occurrence five years later, I doubt whether any of the many demos in Britain's other rugby capitals against the 1969 South African tourists had a local rugby-team leading it. The team at the head of the Cardiff demonstration was Tiger Bay's very own multi-racial team, the CIACS. Wilfred Wooller to this day thinks they were a bunch of students bussed in from North London Polytechnic or Sussex University!

In that invigorating political atmosphere, it was no bad time to serve your apprenticeship. Was it the kind of political activity you would expect in a capital city? Sometimes the chief concerns were international and sometimes British-oriented, sometimes about Cardiff itself. Only occasionally was there a conscious Welsh dimension, as with the question 'Did Welsh rugby operate a colour bar?' There was certainly an unconscious Welsh dimension. I can clearly recall struggling with the design of a poster for our march up Queen Street. We wanted it to read YCH A FI APARTHEID, but we didn't know how to spell Ych a fi. If we spelt it in English as UGHAVEE APARTHEID it didn't look right, but in the strict Welsh it might appear to some monoglot Cardiffians that we could be Afrikaners a long way from home and in favour not against. I think we did both versions in the end side by side, just to make sure.

In my apprenticeship, I can still clearly recall a meeting of the Cardiff Left Club in the back-room of the Old Arcade, still perhaps the quintessential pub in the centre of Cardiff, in which Keith Stuart—now Sir Keith and Chairman of Associated British Ports—lectured the audience, including the young Neil (now the Right Honourable Neil Kinnock) and Jack (now Lord Jack Brooks)—on why productivity in the South Wales coalmines in the 1960s was lower than that of the Polish coal industry in 1937 or some such unutterably depressing statistic. Considering that there were 100,000 miners in Wales at the time, we were discussing big problems looming on the horizon. Little did we realize it then, but the productivity figures of the South Wales Coalfield are looking very healthy now—by the simple method of putting 99,500 miners out of work!

PLOTS AND PLANS

In the lounge bar of that same pub also took place most of the plotting to shape the future of the city-centre. We wanted to resist the take-over of 'our' city-centre by property developers and their many-tentacled consultants. Until the Barrage proposal came along in 1987, I never thought I would see again the intensity of feeling and the high fever of campaigning that swirled around the two big issues of a quarter of a century ago, the Hook

Road and the Ravenseft central shopping-area expansion on Bute Terrace.

Both proposals had their origins in the Colin Buchanan plan for revamping the whole of the central area. The Hook Road was the means for emptying the handbags and wallets of those living in the well-off north Cardiff suburbs into the tills of the new shopping-area on Bute Terrace. The deeper meaning behind the ferocious opposition to those proposals was the people of a city learning how to take control of their own destiny.

Like the powers-that-be on the City Council, we all wanted a central-area expansion for our city that was worthy of a capital city. We wanted the best, just as much as they did. We just did not see how that could possibly be achieved by hauling in flash consultants from London, who had never visited let alone understood our city, and letting them charge outrageous fees for messing up our city-centre. Why couldn't the people of Cardiff themselves run and plan and own their own city? Capital cities, if they wanted to be taken seriously, could not be designed by London consultants, owned by London property companies and full of chain-stores selling identical ranges of goods like shopping-centres everywhere. How could Cardiff be a capital that Wales could be proud of if everything was run from outside?

Apart from the central area, the big issue was Leasehold Reform. Getting that law on Leasehold Enfranchisement passed in 1967-8 prevented the inner ring of Cardiff's older suburbs from falling into decay and eventually slum clearance. Although Tiger Bay had had a film made about it and Loudoun Square, its heart, featured prominently in it, Tiger Bay was not saved from slum clearance. The bottom end of Splott including Robinson Square, which had absolutely none of the redeeming features of Loudoun Square, was not saved from slum clearance. The Wellington Street district of Riverside went the same way. Then the City Council got very cold feet about slum clearance.

The reason was the disgrace of the 'double mortgages'. What happened was that the City Council was very progressive about handing out cheap mortgages to anyone buying their terraced house from the landlord. 'Be a homeowner' was the war-cry.

However, the problem was that the City Treasurer's Department did not make any checks with the Public Health Department. They in turn were condemning some of the newly-mortgaged properties as unfit for human habitation under slum clearance powers. When their homes were demolished, all these new property-owning democrats with shattered dreams would get was about £100 site-value. Then they would have to buy another house, and get a mortgage on that one as well, while still paying a mortgage on the first!

Cardiff's inner-city housing was deterioriating fast in the 1960s. The houses were getting old and were very prone to rising damp, wet rot and dry rot, because of the high water-table. Nobody had much incentive to improve them, because of the threat of slum clearance and their leasehold status. With so much of Cardiff having been built between 1870 and 1914 and buildings usually lasting about a hundred years before they fall down, the old Marquis of Bute's cunning 99-year leases would have had a devastating effect on the shape of the city and its social character. This was particularly true west of the Taff, where Bute's land-ownership had been total. It is hard to imagine what Cardiff would look like today if Leashold Reform had not been got onto the Statute Book in 1968.

Incredible as it may now seem, at the end of the 99-year lease, the house on the plot of ground, and it had to be in good repair too, reverted to the ground landlord. The Marquis of Bute was not around any more, but the company which had inherited his land-owning interests certainly was. It was called Western Ground Rents and this inheritor of the Bute land-interests would have had the choice to sell the land cleared for council tower-blocks or new private housing-estates, which would also have been leasehold, of course. Then the whole 99-year-long not-so-merry-go-round would have started up all over again.

Cardiff was lucky. Cities with a big social problem very rarely get a whole Act of Parliament passed largely for their own benefit. There was, of course, leasehold property elsewhere in Britain, but not on the scale and with the monopoly power that applied in Cardiff. If you had wanted to build a house in Cardiff in the last century, and you didn't want to take a 99-year lease from the Marquis of Bute, you would have had the same problem as trying to buy a red Model T Ford from Henry Ford! The shape of Cardiff's politics and the shape of the city itself were intertwined.

If Leasehold Enfranchisement had not arrived in the nick of time, Cardiff would look totally different today. The inner city suburbs built a century ago, in an arc around from Splott in the east through Roath and Plasnewydd, Cathays to Canton, Riverside and around to Grangetown in the south-west, would be quite unrecognizable. Most of the terraces, both with bay-windows and without, would be gone, to be replaced half by council flats in tower-blocks and half by twee town-houses. Cardiff was narrowly saved from all those late-1960s disasters.

With Leasehold Reform enfranchisement in place and Improvement Grants coming in with the Housing Act of 1969, old inner-city Cardiff had it made. You bought your unimproved terraced house cheap. You bought the freehold, you got a grant and did the house up. You were your own boss—neither dependent on the state nor the Council nor on the Marquis of Bute nor on Western Ground Rents. That was when it seems to me Cardiff really stopped being somebody else's company-town and became a city proper. People could be independent without needing to be wealthy.

The idea of 'a property-owning democracy' came alive on the banks of the Taff long before Margaret Thatcher hit on the slogan. It wasn't quite a property-owning democracy, it was a leasehold-enfranchising, improvement-grant-refurbishing, property-mortgaging democracy. That was how Cardiff was reclaimed for its own citizens and turned into a capital city worthy of the name and with which the rest of Wales could identify.

This was also the era of the Great Cardiff Conservative Councillor Corruption Trial—a trial which started with a Councillor who was Chairman of the Watch (i.e. Police) Committee being arrested at six in the morning and taken to the Police Station in his dressing-gown. It ended in farce, wasting innumerable thousands of man-years of South Wales Fraud Squad time and effort. The judge directed the jury to acquit the Conservative Councillors and their property-developer associates in the dock. The verdict caused much gnashing of teeth among the police, and not only in Cardiff. Big city police-forces up and down the country had a dozen or so similar cases pending, waiting to see how the Cardiff Trial went first.

The trial was therefore a kind of fore runner of the Poulson-Pottinger-T. Dan Smith-Gerald Murphy Swansea and Durham Mafia trials of seven years later. Then the Establishment made a much more determined effort to stamp out corruption in dealings between business and local government. The many jail sentences handed out did not just apply to Labour politicians and one or two council chief officers. It is not every day, after all, that an actual Number One civil servant like Pottinger running a Government Department becomes a guest of Her Majesty.

The Swansea Mafia and the Dan Smith trials in the mid-1970s were fascinating in their way, because they involved the control of the huge house-building budgets of city councils. The abortive Cardiff corruption trial was quite different. It involved in some ways the more important principle of how planning permissions for new office-blocks were agreed. That after all would determine what eventual shape Cardiff would take. Would it be planned, or would it be arranged by 'fixers' in the Members' Room in the City Hall, shelling out the profits on the rising price of land with permission for office blocks, like the swag from a bank-robbery?

As I was a junior town-planner at the time, that farcical trial in Cardiff meant a lot to me. Indeed, during the police investigation and the trial I used to answer the phone in the Planning Department by saying 'City Swindles here, can I help you?' Even though nobody was sent down or even found guilty, the shock-waves of a senior figure on the Watch Committee being arrested for corruption were profound. Acts were undoubtedly cleaned up. Younger councillors who might have been tempted were deterred. Cardiff was spared the later horrors of bent local government. By the time Paddy French started his *Rebecca* scandal-sheet, to expose local corruption, most of the dirt he was digging up came from elsewhere in Wales. If he had started *Rebecca* ten years earlier Cardiff would have been far more fruitful territory.

But it wasn't just me as a town-planner who was worried, and even ashamed of being from Cardiff, when I met other planners in summer schools while the trial was dragging on. The general public in Cardiff was getting very worked-up about the future shape of central Cardiff as well. The plans had been drawn up for the year 2000 by the City Council's big-time planning consultants Sir Colin Buchanan and Partners. Buchanan was a 'roads' man. To him planning a city's future was a simple process. You worked out what the land-uses were going to be. Then you worked out how much road-traffic those buildings and people would need to bring into play. Then you built roads wide enough and long enough to accommodate all the traffic. You knocked down any buildings standing in the way.

Simple enough really, until people got wind of the proposals to build dual-carriageways in front and behind the castle. The one crossing Bute Park was bad enough, but the one planned to run the length of the green in front of the castle caused a huge outcry. It would cut off the city-centre from the front of the castle, reversing most of what had been achieved forty years previously when the view of the castle had been opened up by demolishing the shops on the north side of Castle Street. It released strong forces. It was dynamite. It was political in a way that went way beyond party politics.

It was the clash between the need to venerate your own city's heritage and the desire to be in the big-time as a prestige high-tech modern European capital city with motorways everywhere. Did we really want these new motorways running in front and behind the castle or did we want to build our future around our familiar landmarks, the things that tied us to our past? In a city singularly lacking in landmarks, did it really make sense to knock down the Animal Wall?

Most people in Cardiff, including myself, didn't actually know it as the Animal Wall until the row over its impending demolition broke out, but we had loved that wall from when we were children. It became a battle for the soul of the city—whose city was it in the end? Professor Sir Colin Buchanan might be an enormously important figure in the world of town-planning but did he live here? Did we actually have to listen to him, immensely distinguished though he was, much the most pre-eminent urban traffic expert of his day? Did we have to do what he said? Everyone certainly knew it was called the Animal Wall by the time the controversy was over and the wall was saved. I still find it curious that there is no sign at either end of the wall to tell citizens and tourists alike who designed it and why and when. No matter, the Buchanan and Animal Wall controversy meant that ordinary people in Cardiff were learning to challenge the experts and think things out for themselves.


## THE HOOK-ROAD HORROR

Buchanan and Partners had also proposed a six-lane highway into the city-centre from the expanding northern suburbs ploughing its way through Roath Park, Roath, Plasnewydd and Adamsdown to reach the to-be-expanded central shopping-area. The City Council had swallowed their pride in scrapping most of the maze of motorways in the Buchanan Plan, but this one single proposal survived. The City was determined to build it. General Sherman got a better welcome while marching through Georgia than this Hook Road proposal got in Cardiff east of the Taff. The fight-back was amazing. Although the ruling Conservative Party on the Council was fully committed to it, there were enough Tory rebels willing to join Labour to get within about two votes of over-turning the Hook Road (a bit like the Maastricht Bill!). Along comes a miraculously offered by-election in Penylan, the safest Tory seat on the Council. Half the local Tory Party in Penylan, those living west of Roath Park Lake (where the road would have come through) defect and campaign for the Labour candidate, Mrs Yvette Roblin, and Labour wins Penylan for the first and probably the last time.

This was a sensation! But still not enough to stop the Hook Road. On the actual day of the Council meeting, another Tory, this time a loyal supporter of the Road, gets stuck in an almighty traffic jam on the Treforest Trading Estate on his way back from Merthyr to the City Hall. Labour plus this handful of Tory rebels win the day by a single vote. It's curtains for the Hook Road! That was the most significant vote ever taken in the City Council. The proposal was abandoned just like that, even though all the experts and the entire establishment had affirmed that Cardiff's central area couldn't be modernized without it. Cardiff would choke to death without it. Has it? Did we? Were there horrendous consequences to this popular rebellion against the will of the experts?

No more than there were for keeping the Animal Wall in front of Cardiff Castle. No more than there were a couple of years later when the proposed huge Ravenseft scheme to relocate the city shopping-centre southward to Bute Terrace was dropped as well. The St David's Centre is the Mark II shopping-centre, forced on the property companies and the City Council and its consultants by a campaign of opposition, combined (I have to concede) with the slump brought on by the three-day week, but nevertheless not what 'they' told 'us' we ought to have.

Cardiff had a vaulting ambition to get noticed and accepted back in the First Division of Britain's cities as it did in the Good Old Days of 1870 to 1914. The Ravenseft scheme was supposed to be the key to it. What we got instead, the St David's Centre, is a highly efficient retailing machine, which does fit into the shape of Cardiff. I find it a bit lacking in character and local retailers and I don't like its name. The big plus for it is that it is only there because of a rejection of what the authorities dictated. Cardiff was becoming bit by bit a people's city.


THE BATTLE OF THE WATERFRONT

Much of the political energies of the past fifteen years have been devoted to the argument over how best to redevelop the Docks area of the city. Local government services in Cardiff were split into two in 1973-4, when the city lost its County Borough status. South Glamorgan was responsible for education, social services and highways and the City Council for housing, refuse disposal, the bus services and the collection of rates. Both the new authorities under the political leadership of Jack Brooks in the County and Phil Dunleavy in the City, agreed that the key decision needing to be taken was what to do with the waterfront.

As the County Council was responsible for economic development, it was more inclined to the belief that what Dockland Cardiff needed most was more industry. If you couldn't get more trade through the Docks itself, then why not use some of the area around the wharfs for new factories? The City Council's number one responsibility was housing. It was natural therefore that the leadership was more inclined to believe that an injection of new housing into the Docks was the right way forward. It would rejuvenate the area and reverse the drop in population in South Cardiff. If you represented a waterfront ward, you didn't want your ward to disappear as the result of falling numbers of people.

After the threat to the future of the steel industry became overt in the mid-1970s, the urgency of replacement industry for the thousands of job losses became paramount. That was why the incoming Labour Government under Harold Wilson in 1974 gave Cardiff Development Area status to grant-aid the attraction of new industry. Obviously it had been a big advantage to have Jim Callaghan as a local M.P. and effective Number Two in that Government. His influence, combined with the worries over the grim future of the steel industry, reversed the policy of the Welsh Office. Their policy had up to then been 'Cardiff doesn't need new industry—being the capital of Wales should be enough'.

The recession induced by the Three-Day Week, and the two oil-price shocks of 1973 and 1979, meant that the city could not take all that much advantage of Development Area status. By the early 1980s, after the site of the East Moors steelworks had been cleared, the same argument arose again. The whole of Western Europe was littered with empty factories and idle machinery.

What was the point of throwing public money at the unemployment problems of South Cardiff by building new factories which nobody needed?

If nobody would occupy new factories, could the leisure and service industries fill the gap instead? Should the Docks remain Cardiff's backyard or could it become the city's front garden? This was also the period when the Conservative Government created the London and Merseyside Docklands Development Corporations in the aftermath of the Toxteth riots. Property development and not industrial regeneration was the watchword for these Urban Development Corporations. At the same time, South Glamorgan set off on a slight variant of the UDC solution, retaining much more local political control. It was the Urban Development Grant route, doing a deal with the Welsh Office and Tarmac, one of Britain's biggest property companies.

In return for an £8 million grant, Tarmac would build houses and offices on the Bute East Dock and around the network of little feeder canals. The partnership would create 'a little Venice'. The whole thing was christened Atlantic Wharf. I'm surprised it wasn't St David's Wharf. For the period of the great housing boom of the middle 1980s, it was a roaring success. The industry was removed to Collingdon Road on the Bute West Dock, but some inevitably could not find an alternative home, particularly the more specialized companies making manganese-bronze ships' propellors and so forth. The best of the 'heritage' buildings, the bonded warehouse and the LMS warehouse, were tastefully converted into an architect's office and a hotel.

At the same time the old financial and shipping commerce quarter around Mountstuart Square was slowly coming to life again with the rise of the independent television companies. They were springing up because of the insatiable demands of the new Welsh Fourth Channel Authority, S4C. Its headquarters were in Cathedral Road but the search for cheap flexible studio-space caused the emergence of the Media City of Docklands. Some said it ought to have been called Seedier City instead, but what of it? It was bringing new life to a redundant financial district on the

Docks, just as the best-known of the old shipping companies, Reardon Smith, was sinking beneath the waves.

Was the rise of the media-quarter in Mountstuart Square pointing in the direction of a front garden or backyard, as the real future for Cardiff Bay? Perhaps a bit of both. The media people wanted cheap rents. So you could certainly not put up a new building for them. They could only afford tatty ones. On the other hand, media activities were vaguely glamorous and newsworthy, so the Mountstuart Square media-community was always grabbing public attention.

There was a period in the mid-1980s when you couldn't open a newspaper in Cardiff without reading about SuperTed. It was SuperTed this and SuperTed that. SuperTed had done a co-production deal with Portugal—there was going to be a SuperTed Theme Park in South Wales as big as Disney Land. Media money was going to revitalize South Cardiff and perhaps south Wales as well. It wasn't industry as conventionally defined, but it was jobs. It was recycling what you had, altering it a bit, certainly altering the way we think of our cities' downtown areas and what we use them for. So was Atlantic Wharf.

The problem with the success of Atlantic Wharf was that it gave others some big ideas. When the Conservative Government was setting up the second wave of Urban Development Corporations in 1986, Nicholas Edwards, the Secretary of State, decided that Wales must have one too. Its job would be to redevelop the rest of the Dockland untouched so far by Atlantic Wharf. The scale of what he dreamt up, along with his fellow-dreamers from the London estate agents, Jones, Lang and Wootton, was staggering, ten times the size of Atlantic Wharf. If achieved, it would equal the huge work of transformation carried out by the Third Marquis in building the Bute West and East Docks, straightening out the course of the Taff and reconstructing Cardiff Castle.

There were two enormous differences. The first was that the Third Marquis of Bute's schemes on the Docks were called forth by the discovery of coal in the Valleys and the technological changes in transport, both in railway haulage and ships' motive-power. The Cardiff Bay scheme was all on spec. Second, the Marquis was risking his own money. Nicholas Edwards required the taxpayer to fork out hundreds of millions of pounds, while he risked nothing—not even his political reputation. He was already committed to retiring from being Secretary of State and a member of the House of Commons at the 1987 Election. It looked more like a retirement gift to himself, paid for by the taxpayer, than anything else.

No one doubted the need to bring new economic life to the Docks, or to generate a higher standard of living for those living in the waterfront and steelworks communities. The argument was over the need to turn the destiny of a city over to an unelected authority to do it. They in turn would turn it over to an army of estate agents and consultants, whose main qualification was that they could not point Cardiff out on a map of the British Isles. Preferably, they should also not be able to point Wales out on a map of the British Isles.

It was the biggest army of invasion by invitation since the splurge of consultants' contracts handed out by the City Council a quarter of a century previously: Colin Buchanan and partners, Ravenseft and their estate agents—it was the same kind of people. The same kind of solutions bearing no relation to how Cardiff actually functioned as a city were being offered. We had seen it all before. The barrage was a kind of marine equivalent of the Hook Road, the Ravenseft shopping-precinct on Bute Terrace with adjoining giant car-park all rolled into one. No attempt was made to pretend that this was a scheme which fitted in to downtown Cardiff as it was. It was not intended to fit.

That was its supreme virtue, according to its promoters. It was visionary, not evolutionary. It was something totally different. It would sweep away the industry from the West Dock area, even the industry that had only just been shifted there to make way for houses and offices at Atlantic Wharf. Collingdon Road, the main drag of the Bute West Dock area, and with more welding-shops than Venice had gondolas, was to become a Mall linking the Bay with the City Centre. This was the front garden strategy with a vengeance. It would revolutionize Cardiff's prospects—if it worked, that is. Or else it would turn Cardiff into a de-industrialized wasteland.

The biggest difference between this new army of consultants and estate agents and the ones hired in the 'sixties was that the City Council was open to pressure from the voters—the Urban Development Corporation was not. So long as it had the confidence of the Secretary of State, it was almost untouchable. This time there could be no Penylan by-election in the nick of time to save us from this Hook Road-in-the-Water. Would it pass the test of bringing new economic life to the Docks and a higher standard of living to the local residents? Initially it failed that test.

Cardiff Bay and its consultants were so anxious to produce world-class designs for the new Cardiff Bay waterfront that they bought every scrap of land in the Docks they could and simply took it off the market for three years. They needed those three years just to draw up plans. These plans included giving the old, still empty East Moors steelworks industrial site the title of Ocean Park. Even more fancy, the stretch of new road along the Tremorfa foreshore from the Central Sewer Outfall past the mountains of scrap waiting to be remelted in the steelworks, on past the furnace-slag dump as far as the Eastern Sewer Outfall, was to be called the Corniche. I suppose the French Riviera has a sewer outfall or two as well, but Corniche was going it a bit, I thought.

The problem was that this period of land sterilization coincided with the property boom of the late 1980s. By the time Cardiff Bay was ready to release the land the property boom was over, to be replaced by the worst slump in fifty years.

What about the standard of living of local people? Will the acid comment of James Baldwin on property-led redevelopment in North America's big cities turn out to be true of the new Tiger Bay too? He wrote, 'Urban Renewal equals Negro Removal'. It had better not, but the warning is there. If North America's big city urban renewal experience has nothing to teach us, why have so many hundreds of those connected with the Cardiff Bay scheme been flown to Baltimore to see the Inner Harbour scheme?

As the word SuperTed dropped out of the vocabulary of local newspapers, the word Baltimore and 'Inner Harbour' took its place. If you hadn't been there, you were obviously a nobody. This North American model-city was not the old port that was so well known to W. H. Davies, the Newport poet-tramp. Nor was it any more the port from which Eugene O'Neill set out on his journeys as a seaman to Cardiff. This was the new tourist, yacht-owner and PR executive's Baltimore—the Baltimore of the 'Civic Booster', who wanted to take a shabby traditional port-city out of its obscurity into the 'good news' sunlight.

Cardiff Bay was intended and planned as a mongrel, cross-bred by Baltimore Inner Harbour out of London Docklands. By the time the canary had died at Canary Wharf, the Bay Development Corporation conveniently invented a new justification for producing no jobs during the boomlet of the late 1980s. They claimed that they had been busy learning from the London Dockland Corporation's mistakes. They never answered the fundamental questions, For whose benefit? At whose behest? Accountable to whom? Who had a power of veto? Was the strategy of 'High Price and High Class' workable? Does revitalizing an area mean raising the rent or getting something going inside the buildings you've got? If you are a property surveyor, only the first will do. The barrage scheme had to raise the rent levels dramatically. That was how the barrage was supposed to be paid for, in theory anyway.

There are probably just two ways of redeveloping Cardiff Docklands. The first is to allow the city centre to expand southwards from the bottom of St. Mary Street taking it under the main-line railway down towards the Pier Head. The other is to start at the Pier Head and Mountstuart Square and then to roll up the carpet northwards, up Bute Street to the city centre. The problem with the second method is that the danger of Cardiff's continuing to be the Tale of Two Cities will still be there. The argument for it is that Cardiff has historically had this unusual dumb-bell shape, with two commercial centres. Can the 1870 pattern be repeated in the 1990s, but without the coal trade?

The problem with the barrage idea is that it pins everything on to the 'Start at the Pier Head and work northwards' strategy. Once the retiring Nicholas Edwards had tied himself and the Government to it, there could be no rational comparisons of the two ways of doing the job. Everything, including the Government's face in Wales, was being pinned on one giant piece of masonry. Its sole purpose is to create Cardiff's very own Lake Woe-begun. The significance of the lake for the barrage promoters is almost mystic. With a lake Cardiff will get 30,000 jobs, without a lake it won't. 'It is the absence of a freshwater lake that is holding back the arrival of 30,000 jobs in Cardiff'. That was the Ark of the Covenant. That was the Big Idea formed in Nicholas Edwards's head as he stood on the top of Penarth Head with his estate agent consultant from Mayfair. You either believed it or you didn't. If you didn't you were opposed to 'progress'. You were a Fluddite, in effect.

The lake may become the Eighth Wonder of the World or it may become the world's largest ever bowl of Brown Windsor soup. About a third of the flow of the Taff and the Ely in a dry July or August is treated sewage from the Valleys. It's all processed at the Treatment Works at Cilfynydd on the Taff and Rhiwsaeson on the Ely. The water entering the lake is going to be a reminder of the organic interdependence of Cardiff and the Valleys. The Garden City on the plains will be connected, oh so intimately, with its hard-working Valley hinterland, because Cardiff's beautiful amenity lake will have been through at least one set of kidneys in the Valleys before it gets to the city. In fact, on those occasions when the odd dead cow falls into the river and floats down into the bay, I suppose it could luxuriate in the name of Lake Steak and Kidneys!

One of the other curiosities of modern sewage treatment is that it can't remove oestrogen, the stuff of which birth-control pills are made. You can therefore expect a significant build-up of indestructible female hormone in the lake behind the barrage in summer, when rainwater flows are at minimum levels. The more women in the Valleys use the pill, the more likely it is that macho yachtsmen and oarsmen who fall into the lake in Cardiff and swallow a mouthful or two of water will not need to shave as often as they did before. These are uncharted waters of social change we are moving into. This is the new Wales. Ex-coal-miners now take the kids to school, while their wives go out to work as bread-winners at the local electronics factory. Hairy-chested water-sportsmen in Cardiff become more smooth-skinned, the harder they train in the Bay.

Let us forget Nicholas Edwards's watery ambitions to become the next Marquis of Bute at the taxpayer's expense. A lot of redevelopment of Dockland Cardiff can go ahead now regardless of the barrage. What is the potential of the Pier Head area of Cardiff? It undoubtedly is capable of becoming a huge tourist attraction on a par with Liverpool's Albert Dock area. In any area, if enough public money is poured in to create the tourist attractions, it can bring in a million visitors a year. Liverpool has done it with its Pier Head. Cardiff undoubtedly could as well. The Pier Head needs the trebling of the size of the Welsh Industrial and Maritime Museum. It needs the Techniquest Hands-on Science experience to be finished and given a permanent home. It could do with something like a Roald Dahl Children's Museum around the Norwegian Seaman's Church, a few galleon restaurants moored in the dock, and perhaps the new Opera House. Perm any four from five and you have a tourist industry for all seasons. It would build on the wondrous Docks Board Headquarters Building and the partial success of the new Boardwalk. I say partial because they fractured the Butetown Main Sewer under the Boardwalk when they built the supports for it. You don't half know it at low tide.

The Opera House has been designated as the 'gift' that Wales will get from the Millennium Fund part of the National Lottery proceeds. Someone has decided that already. I don't know who. It's been done behind closed doors. If we say we want something else instead, we are warned that we will finish up with nothing. 'That's what you're having and that's it!' It would have been nicer if we had been asked. The Welsh Establishment are very keen on the Welsh National Opera, there are no two ways about that. In fact, membership of either the Board or the League of

Friends of the Welsh National Opera is practically a membership ticket for the Inner Sanctum of the Welsh Establishment.

It is almost a parallel to Lord Victor Rothschild's dictum about the British Establishment. The sort of 'Good Chaps' deemed fit to serve on Royal Commissions, according to his theory, was that they should be aged 53, white Anglo-Saxon males resident in the south-east of England and members of the Reform Club. In Wales, they should be 53, white, Welsh, but not too Welsh, resident in, or owning second homes in the Vale of Usk and members of the Board of the National Opera! Would the people of Wales have set a permanent home for the Opera Company as their top priority if they had been asked? I doubt it, because the Company has never managed to move opera nearer the people, certainly not to the people of Cardiff, who are its hosts.

Now if the Welsh National Opera had put on a performance of *Carmen* in the Freeman's cigar factory, it might break that barrier down between the cultural and political élite and the ordinary citizenry. After all, *Carmen* is about women working in a tobacco factory. You've got a choice of two in Cardiff. You could perform it in the old factory in North Clive Street, or in the new one in Penarth Road. That way, you can persuade ordinary people that opera is about them too. If it's about them, then they might be persuaded that it's for them too. The effort that has gone into building up the Opera Company into the emblem of Welsh excellence is phenomenal. It has pretty well taken the place of the national rugby-team as the one thing that we Welsh can excel in, at which we are better than the English.

Perhaps really that is what this operatic obsession is all about. The English Establishment were never very happy about their inability to get anywhere near Wales at rugby in the 1960s and 1970s. Rugby Union is after all the game of the Establishment in England and is classless in Wales. Wales beating England at rugby is striking a blow for equality; it is not just winning a game, it is rubbing the noses of the Establishment in it.

Opera singing is entirely different. It is something that the Establishment permits us to be good at. We have their full permission. Why? As far as the English upper classes are concerned, the Welsh can excel at opera precisely because it doesn't challenge the established order. The powers that be sit in the audience and shout Bravo and Encore. The performance is done for them and not to them as in rugby. The English Establishment have a much more comfortable relationship with the troublesome Principality next door, now that we are deemed to be a world centre of excellence at something entirely unthreatening like opera. It has made us Welsh Establishment-friendly.

If the people of Wales were given the choice between producing a wonderful opera company or wonderful rugby teams, I have little doubt what the choice would be. Why should we worry whether we are user-friendly to the Establishment? They are obviously going to look more kindly on Wales, now that we have temporarily lost our superiority over England at the one key sport, which signifies an expensive private education. Playing rugger at public school is a preparation for being in charge of the country. It is not our job in Wales to help the English Establishment recover its self-confidence after the loss of Empire. Let us therefore decide our own priorities for Welsh national excellence.

The new Opera House at the Pier Head is being touted as doing for the Cardiff waterfront what the Sydney Opera House has done for Sydney and Australia during the past quarter of a century. Whether it will prove to be a world-famous landmark in that category remains to be seen. The new Lake Woe-begun behind the barrage and the new Opera House are meant to signify the new southward and seaward shift of the direction of development of the city. After a hundred years of spreading out fan-shaped from the city centre and the Docks, west, east and north, the city is now meant to try to implode back in on itself and choose the one direction for growth it has not so far used this century.

# DEVELOPMENT OF A EURO-CAPITAL

From the building of the Bute West Dock in 1840 to that of the Queen Alexandra Dock just before the outbreak of the First World War, Cardiff developed in a seaward direction and moved its centre of gravity south. A whole new shoreline two miles south of the natural shore was created. After the Great War things were different. You couldn't go south any more. Cardiff expanded out across the river Ely. From 1920 to 1950 the city developed westward and built the sprawling Ely council estate, bigger than all but the seven largest Welsh towns. From 1950 onwards the city crossed the Rhymney and expanded north-eastwards. It developed the Llanrumney, Rumney, Trowbridge and now St Mellon's estates, as well as Llanedeyrn and Pentwyn. Between these two giant council estates the east-west spread of Cardiff has doubled from three-and-a-half miles to seven.

While these two huge lobes of municipal housing were being built east and west into the Vale of Glamorgan and Monmouthshire, the city's private suburbia was spreading north towards Caerphilly Mountain. That is a very formidable barrier to urban sprawl. In fact, Cardiff has sharply defined natural geographical limits to its expansion in three out of the four directions. As marked as the Caerphilly Mountain barrier to the north is Tumble Hill and Leckwith Hill to the west, and of course the sea to the south. The only direction which Cardiff can take for easy unobstructed growth is north-east up the Lower Rhymney Valley and east along the coastal plain. This could eventually in fifty years give us an urbanized coalescence along the coast, called either Carport or Newdiff. Not an appealing prospect, but that's where all the pressure for housing development is coming from.

It's certainly not an inviting prospect for Newport. If Cardiff Bay Development Corporation succeed in their strategy of changing the Bay from being Cardiff's backyard to being its front garden, then there can be no doubt where all the backyard functions are going to go—to the banks of the Usk. Newport has already lost a worrying amount of its function as a regional shopping-centre for the whole of Monmouthshire to a combination of Cwmbrân and Cardiff. It's gone that way because of the increasing use of the private car and reduced dependence on bus and train. Newport in this particular future will be in danger of becoming the Gateshead to Cardiff's Newcastle or the Birkenhead to Cardiff's Liverpool or, worst of all, the Oakland to Cardiff's San Francisco. And we all remember what Gertrude Stein said about Oakland—'There's no there there!' Not much fun either for Cardiff to be known as the Latin Quarter of Newport.

That is my worst fear about the impact of Cardiff Bay on Cardiff. It could lead to de-industrializing what little industry we have left in the city. When the steel industry in Cardiff was being fought for in the late 1970s, the argument we used was that we did have the largest steel re-rolling complex in Europe here. Therefore it made sense to have a steelworks to feed it. We got our new steelworks. Now if Cardiff Bay is to become de-industrialized through increasing land values, or the front garden obsession, Allied Steel might be forced to move the re-rolling complex up to Scunthorpe, where they assuredly do not suffer from any kind of front garden obsession.

## THE LONG ENGAGEMENT

When Cardiff started building the Llanrumney council estate on the east bank of the Rhymney River in 1950, it was moving into Monmouthshire. By the time Cardiff was declared the capital of Wales in 1955, it was in the odd position of expanding at a rapid rate into an area which was not properly part of Wales. Monmouthshire was shared between Wales and England. All official documents had to refer to Wales and Monmouthshire to have any legal effect in that singular county. Newport RFC was affiliated to the English Rugby Union as well as the WRU. If this 'Wales and Mon.' legal anomaly had not been corrected a little later on, Cardiff would be in a very strange position now for the capital of Wales. A fifth of its population would be living in a county officially half in and half out of Wales. Regardless of whether the green belt between Cardiff and Newport is protected, that twenty per cent is undoubtedly going to grow. It is the cheapest and possibly the only way the city can grow.

Since the completion of the huge council estate in Ely in 1950, Cardiff has inexorably grown north-eastward. First Llanrumney and Rumney, then Llanedeyrn and Pentwyn, then Trowbridge and St Mellon's. Now north Pentwyn. Although there has been more suburbanization of the south side of Caerphilly Mountain too around Thornhill, you know that has to stop pretty soon, when the mountain slopes get too steep. By contrast there is nothing to stop the centre of gravity of Cardiff moving further and further east, no natural obstacles setting a limit, once you've crossed the river Rhymney. That leaves the question open on what the employment base of this direction of expansion is going to be. We have already seen an explosion of riots affect Ely on the west side in 1991, when that estate had largely lost its original employment base.

It also leaves open the question as to whether Cardiff should grow much more. How would such expansion affect its relationship with the rest of Wales? What are the people of the rest of Wales looking for in their capital? Are they looking for political leadership and an evolution towards democratic decision making? Are they looking for financial and technological expertise? Are they looking for landmarks and trophy buildings, national institutions which are symbols of Wales's achievements? Are they looking for posh restaurants serving culinary specialities or maybe a red light district when they visit? Or are they just looking for the rugby stadium?

Do the people of Wales want a city larger than the present Cardiff of 290,000? A Cardiff eventually merging with Newport would be about half a million. It would be bigger than Bristol. Is that desirable or significant? Is Cardiff too small at less than 300,000 to be a proper Euro-capital, which cannot look other Euro-capitals in the eye because of its lack of numbers? As it is at present, it is roughly in the same size league as Helsinki and Oslo. Finland and Norway have about the same population as Wales with four million rather than our three. It would be very much smaller than Copenhagen or Barcelona, which each have over a million residents. You can find comparable Euro-capitals, however you measure Cardiff's present and future numbers.

Looking at Cardiff's future from the point of view of the modern American Civic Booster, for whom all growth must be a Good Thing, you could easily envisage a crescent of unbroken urban-suburban development stretching all the way from Cardiff Wales Airport at Rhoose, a dozen miles west of City Hall, right across through Barry, Cardiff and Newport to the Llanwern Steelworks in the east. It would have a population count of around 550,000 by the turn of the millennium. Barry would have merged into Dinas Powys, which would in turn have joined Penarth. Penarth would have slid into Cardiff Bay.

The gap between the eastern edge of Cardiff beyond today's St Mellon's and the western edge of Newport beyond today's Duffryn would be down to half a mile. It is only four miles now. Passing that gap on the 125 train takes less than two minutes; I've measured it. Would that sort of big (for us) capital be seen as a powerhouse or engine-room for Wales, or would it be seen as a Fat Capital sucking all the talent, energy and resources out of the rest of Wales? A Fat Cats capital, much too big for its boots perhaps?

What is the right relationship between Cardiff and the rest of Wales? I remember asking a fellow-student who was from Llannerch-y-medd, in the middle of Anglesey, well over two hundred miles and a comfortable six-hour journey from Cardiff, 'What do you think of Cardiff? Do you think of it as your capital city?' I was trying to put myself in the shoes of a Cardiffian who found that the capital of Wales was in Rhyl, say. I was quite pleasantly surprised to hear him say that he was very proud of walking around the streets, thinking to himself, 'I'm Welsh—this is my capital city'. What is the real nature of the tie behind that bald statement?

Cardiff is the political, emotional and sporting capital of Wales, with its 2.9 million people. It shares the status of being the political capital of Wales with London and is very much the junior partner. It is the commercial service capital for industrial South Wales, a region of two million people, a function it shares with Swansea, but with Cardiff the senior partner. Third, it is the shopping and commuter capital of south-east Wales, the sub-region where fully half the population of Wales lives within twenty-five miles of the city. It shares this function with Newport, but again it is the senior partner. Finally, it is the place of residence of 290,000, exactly 10% of the Welsh total. Those are the four facets of the Cardiff-Wales engagement.

I think that Cardiff has a much weaker grip on the first and second of those facets than on the third. Cardiff's great bulwark is its relationship with the Valleys and its strengthening ties with Gwent. That is the historic reason why Cardiff became the largest city in Wales and it is still what we do best. It is what we rely on for our bread and butter. The Valleys are so Welsh, it helps to Welshify Cardiff too. The industrial valleys of Mid Glamorgan and Gwent may not be Welsh in language, but they are the archetypal Wales with a culture that nobody fails to recognize. For half the population of Wales to be living in Cardiff or reasonable commuting distance really establishes it as the unavoidable choice as capital.

One of the peculiarities of modern Wales is that Cardiff's easy dominance of Welsh life is bound to become more and more difficult to sustain. We have had it far too easy as a capital. Not only did half the population of Wales live within 25 miles of the city, but over two-thirds of the total Welsh population lived in a solid and homogeneous zone of development in industrial South Wales. If you were the leading city of industrial South Wales you were just about certain to be the capital of Wales. That is now going to be less and less true as time goes by. The population of the industrial south is not growing; it is barely stable.

The growing areas of Wales are in Clwyd and Dyfed, with a little in mid-Wales as well. It is not economic growth that is going to take the population of Wales over the three-million mark for the first time ever, shortly after the turn of the millennium on present trends. It is retirement and lifestyle migration into north and west Wales, combined with commuter spill-over from Cheshire into Clwyd. The 70% of Wales' population living in the industrial south only a few years ago will have dropped to 60% soon after the year 2000. The new Wales, as you might call it, is much less likely to show unquestioning allegiance to Cardiff as the capital, if Cardiff isn't doing the job that Wales needs. This is simply because the expanding areas are a long way from Cardiff. It's the unavoidable fact of Welsh geography.

Even in carrying out the function of exercising the commercial and industrial leadership of industrial South Wales, serious weaknesses are already apparent. The job of providing the scientific, technological, financial, medical and trading leadership has been eroded ever since the decline in the coal export trade. The confidence that Cardiff then had has never been recovered. Some even argue that the Severn Bridge has made things worse. It is more likely that it was built decades too late. What is certainly true is that you can hardly make an insurance claim in South Wales now without finding that it's going to be processed in Bristol.

It is also worrying that the number of companies of any consequence with headquarters or research laboratories in the Cardiff area is so pathetically small. There is Allied Steel and there are the two privatized utilities, Welsh Water and South Wales Electricity. So many of the middle-sized Welsh firms that used to have headquarters in Cardiff, such as Avana Bakeries, A.B. Electronics, Aberthaw Cement, and John Williams, have been swallowed up by take-overs or receivers.

In the world of science, technology and medicine the tradition is thin and the present not all that much better. Looking back at what Commander Willows did with the early airships, and Marconi's successful but short sojourn in the area for his radio experiments with radio, it does not amount to a huge contribution to putting Wales on the map. More recently Brian Josephson became one of the youngest ever Nobel Prize winners for physics, but he got it working at the Cavendish Laboratories in Cambridge. I often wonder how the authorities in Cardiff would handle an opportunity of leadership in an exciting area of scientific or medical advance, with incalculable prospects. Would they fluff it, or be frightened of it, or would they show the vision to mobilize the resources to develop and support it?

We might quite easily have been the leading heart-transplant centre of Europe. After all, Magdi Yacoub did much of his early training as a cardiac surgeon in Sully and Llandough Hospital. He was then turned down for a consultant's job here. That is how he finished up in Harefield, a clapped-out complex of Nissen huts in the middle of Middlesex. Did the top brass of the Health Authority turn him down because they were plain stupid, too stupid to recognize they had the world's best heart surgeon on offer to them? Or was it the very fact that they did realize that this guy was going to go all the way to the top that put them off? Were they scared because they realized that they would have to handle all the problems that go with being world-leaders in any field? Are we in Cardiff afraid of excellence? Do we suffer from delusions of mediocrity? If you are afraid of excellence, you can't be a real capital city.

As it happens, we are currently looking at a perhaps similar opportunity to prove our mettle. Although the last twenty years have been characterized as the age of the Silicon Chip, the next generation of materials—faster, lighter and tougher than silicon—are gradually taking over. Where are they being researched? Where are they also, thank God, being manufactured? The answer to the first is in Cardiff University. The answer to the second is in St Mellon's, probably with many of John Redwood's favourite class of people working on the production-line. What will come of it? Can the different bits of the jigsaw puzzle be put together that we need to make Cardiff the world technology capital of the post-silicon era? The answer is a great deal more important to Wales than whether we have a barrage or an opera house.

The other function we are only half carrying out is that of being the political capital of Wales. There is no problem over the sporting and emotional capital bits and pieces. The problem is over political decisions. Who makes those decisions and who has the power to veto them? Not the voters of Wales, that's for sure.

That has to affect how Wales as a whole looks up to Cardiff, or not, as the case may be.

All capital cities by their very function generate tensions between the residents of the capital and the citizens of the country at large. Capital cities are all seen as being inhabited by the cats who ran off with the cream and simultaneously botched the running of the country. The voters of countries as small as Ireland and as large as the USA are always moaning about 'the mess in Washington' or its equivalent.

What is unusual about the tensions generated in Cardiff and about Cardiff in the rest of Wales is that they relate to the voters of another country. Who is shutting down all our steelworks and coal-mines? On whose say-so was it that we had to have a barrage? Who says we have to have opt-out schools and hospitals? Who is going to protect us against these impositions? All those lovely Imperial-style civic buildings made out of Portland stone in that Cathays Park, but none of them can stop THEM doing all those things to US. 'What use is it to us? That civic centre is so beautifully laid out, you could easily forget it's dead, politically stone dead'.

Cardiff must have a share of those key decisions if it is to develop as a capital. That is when it will start to emerge on the stage as a Euro-capital, when it is taking or at the very least, sharing in Euro-capital-type decisions. That is when the rest of Wales will start to appreciate its capital city, when Cardiff can deliver the goods for Wales.

We have to over-emphasise the surface trappings of capital city status—the St David's Hall and Shopping Centre, the Cathays Park civic centre, the headquarters of the privatized utilities—precisely because there is so thin a veneer of political and industrial activity under that surface. Surface trappings are all we've got. Where's the beef? you might say. Euro-capital status means about as much as Back to Basics. If we were not covering up the lack of a share in power over the key decisions affecting Wales, we could concentrate more on Cardiff's true heritage as a city. That is when we could start thinking about calling St David's Hall the Bassey-Novello Hall. Cardiff would then stop being the unknown capital. We could concentrate on building up our city's own heritage, if we were not so anxious to paste over the cracks. Politically speaking, we are only a pretend capital.

Nationalists will argue until the cows come home that a share in the big political decisions affecting Wales is not enough. I believe that a big share is what suits the shape and size of Wales best. This is simply because our economy and history are so interwoven with those of England. Wales has kept its separate identity, only because it is so difficult a country to travel around. Cultural influences from elsewhere take a long time to penetrate across the mountains and valleys. The other side of that coin is that Wales has never been an easy country to unite. 'Pleidiol wyf i'm plwyf' would be a much more accurate line in our national anthem than 'pleidiol wyf i'm gwlad'. Loyalty to the parish is more powerful than loyalty to our country. If it were easy to travel from north to south and east to west in Wales, we would be a much more united country, but we would have lost the Welsh language several hundred years ago. We might therefore not be recognizable as Wales at all. It was only the Welsh language that kept our separate identity until we started playing football against England in the 1880s.

Having some kind of elected body giving the people of Wales a say and democratically accountable to them alone would make Cardiff a proper capital. It would also release us from the burden of papering over that democratic deficiency in our system. Cardiff, released from those needs, would be able to breathe as a city. What would we do differently if we could breathe as a city? We could try to give more prominence to those questions that visitors ask out of curiosity as they walk around the city centre.

Who built the Animal Wall and why? Can you climb to the top of St John's Church tower? Can you do a tour of Brain's Brewery? Why do people play baseball in the summer? Can you actually ask to see the Book of Aneirin, one of the world's oldest books of poetry, in the Central Library? Which are William Burges' best buildings and can you see inside them? Why do we have so many arcades? Where is or was the H.Q. of the Taff Vale Railway, whose legal action against the rail union led to the founding of the Labour Party? Why did Disraeli stay at the Cow and Snuffers in Llandaf North? Why did Lionel Walden and Graham Sutherland come to Cardiff to do their paintings of steelworks and docks? How did the National Museum come to have Renoir's *La Parisienne* hanging on the wall—perhaps the most famous painting of a woman in the world after the Mona Lisa?

*La Parisienne* is a kind of cross between the Mona Lisa and Princess Diana. I think we should be making much more of her. Millions of posters and tea-towels, paper plates and souvenirs of all kinds imprinted with the picture should be on sale in every tourist shop and department store in the city. It's a pity that it's not *La Cardiffienne* but you can't have everything. It was purchased with Rhondda coal money. So was much of Cardiff. So that makes *La Parisienne* one of us. We should tell every school-kid growing up in Cardiff all these whys and wherefores, so that they understand their heritage. Likewise it is difficult to get the answers to these questions, if you are a visitor. We are not geared up to explain, only to try to impress.

In the foyer-gallery on the first floor of the City Hall, you might have expected to see some of these questions answered. All you have instead is statues of Henry Tudor, Owain Glyndŵr, Dafydd ap Gwilym and other figures from distant Welsh history who had very little to do with Cardiff. We need to tell the Cardiff Story somewhere. Part of it needs to be inside in a municipal museum of some kind. The old Central Library would almost certainly have to play a part in answering that need. It could answer some of those questions I listed above. It could also explain how it was that in the second half of the 1920s Cardiff City and Huddersfield Town were the Manchester United and Liverpool of the day. Cardiff RFC in the 1947-53 period, inspired by Bleddyn Williams, and Cardiff Amateur Athletic Club in the 1960s with Lynn Davies at the helm, enjoyed equal success to the soccer team's 1920s feats culminating in winning the F.A. Cup in 1927. Indeed, it was called the English Cup until it was won by Cardiff.

Some of the story has to be told outside. Cathedral Road is one of Britain's finest streets, a complete statement about Edwardian architecture. Unfortunately, there are half-a-dozen modern matchbox office-blocks dotted around the town end, which ruin the unity, and therefore its value to our heritage. We should perhaps persuade all the doctors in private practice in Cathedral Road to chip in ten per cent of their fees until we can buy up the modern buildings, surgically remove and replace them with reconstructions in the proper style of Cardiff in its Edwardian heyday. Then we would have a street to show visitors from Llannerch-y-medd to Lhasa.

If we in Cardiff were more conscious of our heritage and knew what appealed to us about it, it would be so much easier to persuade others that it might appeal to them as well. Can we export our pride in what we have? We think it is an uphill task, but is it that difficult? It's an old saying of traders in Cardiff that 'you can't give away a pint of Brain's in Newport'. Wales is a parochial kind of country with all these hills impeding trade, transport and inter-marriage.

The ordinary life of the city is also in a way a story that still needs telling. The media in Cardiff are a major presence, but we have yet to see a decent soap, or cops-and-robbers, or hospital saga in the English language which presents life in general but with Cardiff as the backdrop. No Spender, Boon or Taggart as yet. The Welsh élite would probably prefer to keep off the screen any programme which highlights 'big city' life in Cardiff. They would see it as doing damage to the image of Wales. It's rather like the row over the forecourt and approach to Cardiff Central Station. We all know it looks like a non-stop branch meeting of Lada Drivers Anonymous. Does this make a bad first impression on business visitors? Maybe. So do we scrap all the Ladas or is it better to convert it into part of the Cardiff story—make jokes and folk-songs about it? Maybe even a TV Series called Lada City?

All big cities generate a crime problem and Cardiff is no exception. It is plainly daft to pretend that a cops-and-robbers TV series about Cardiff would drag the good name of Wales in the mud. English-language TV series set in Wales are usually about country vets, rural district nurses on bikes, country doctors and west Wales lifeboat crews—never about urban Wales. The cities of Wales are only tolerated. They are not considered a proper part of Wales. They do exist, but they cannot possibly present the right image of Wales to the outside world. When we do have a cops-and-robbers TV series set in Wales, it will more than likely be called Pwllheli Vice!

I was recently asked by an American congressman from Nebraska 'Is there a Cardiff Sound?' I was baffled at first. Then he explained, 'You know—like the Mersey Beat'. There are a lot of similarities between Cardiff and Liverpool, I explained, but no Cardiff Sound. We are not big enough to make a sound. A real metropolis is supposed to make an occasional contribution to the development of popular music, if only for a short period. The three most prominent pop musicians or groups from Cardiff did have a flurry of fame, but have spent twenty years suing each other over royalties ever since. The Cardiff Sound is lawyers' cash-tills ringing. Maybe it is still Shirley Bassey and Shakin' Stevens, but their musical styles owe nothing to Cardiff.

Where are the blue plaques on the walls of the houses of our best-known citizens apart from Ivor Novello? Where are the plaques for Radmilovic, Driscoll, Bush, Hancock, Bassey, Willows, Josephson, Conrad, O'Neill, Abse, Rubens and Thomas? Thomas? What's someone called Thomas doing in there amidst that cosmopolitan galaxy? Well, R. S. Thomas is justifiably famous and comes from Cardiff. He may wish he came from deepest Llanfihangel-yng-Nghinmeirch, Garndolbenmaen or even Troedrhiwfuwch. But he doesn't. He comes from Cardiff.

Perhaps that sums up the special relationship. There is this suspicion that Cardiff is not Welsh enough to be its true capital. Cardiff is very cosmopolitan and almost American in its population mixture. There are as many McCarthys and Cohens in its telephone directory as there are Llewelyns. It is not that far from the Severn Bridge, maybe forty minutes away. It is definitely in the south-east corner of Wales and not in the middle. It is a border city as well as a seaport and a melting-pot.

But what is Wales? Is the rest of Wales a culturally homogeneous tightly-bound whole?

Is Wales itself all that Welsh, in the traditional cultural sense? Eighty per cent of the population of Wales lives within fifty miles of the English border and is hugely affected by its magnetic pull. That is the big difference in the shape of Wales and Scotland. Eighty per cent of the population of Scotland lives in the middle of Scotland; nobody lives near the border with England. Scotland is a centrepetal country; Wales is the reverse. Wherever you are in Wales, it is easier to get to the adjoining bit of England of the same latitude than to the adjoining area of Wales of the same longitude. If the capital did not reflect this Border Country special character of Wales, it could not do its job half as well. It could not be Wales' window to the rest of the world. It is a Border Capital for a Border Country.

Cardiff's evolution as the capital in the future must be true to this unique character of the England-Wales relationship. Separation would be physically impossible. Offa's Dyke is only a yard high; let's not pretend it's the Irish Sea or the Cheviot Hills. On the other hand, since Wales has hung onto its distinctive traditions through the centuries, in spite of the absence of political decision-making, it would be a crying shame to get homogenized into a mid-Atlantic mish-mash now. Cardiff has a special job to do in taking Wales forward in a way that is distinct but not separate.

At first sight it sounds like an impossible job of tightrope-walking. But it can't be all that difficult. That is what Barcelona and Stuttgart have that we don't. The status of sharing political control that Cardiff and Wales both need is not very different from what the American, Canadian or Australian states have now. Closer to home the Land Governments of Federal Germany already have something close to what we need. Spain after the death of Franco probably provides the closest parallel. The regional Land Governments within Germany don't have different languages and cultures to deal with, as Spain and Britain do. Catalonia and the Basque Country share that special factor and inheritance with Wales and Scotland. The big difference between us and Spain is that Catalonia and the Basque Country are the most advanced regions in Spain in the economic and technological sense. Even in their wildest moments of fantasy the P.R. whizz-kids of the W.D.A. would not claim that about Wales.

We are coming from behind relative to the rest of the UK. Perhaps it is easier to assert the right to a share of political control if you do not feel in the beggars can't be choosers position. Can Cardiff help to provide the technological leadership and the financial services that ought to go with a hefty chunk of political self-determination? Can Cardiff ever be the real capital of Wales without it?

You don't get political self-determination, shared or otherwise, from a load of quangos and a Secretary of State in all his pomp in the Crown Buildings in Cathays Park. The real decisions for the quangos are all made in the Treasury in Whitehall. They are not accountable to the people of Wales, in part or in whole. A capital with the headquarters of all the quangos in the world cannot be the same as a capital which has a focus for the people in it, with real democratic accountability. A democratic Assembly, Senate or Parliament is not only good for the people at large and the politicians whose backsides the people want to kick from time to time. It is good for business, finance, science and technology as well, because it will be the place where real decisions are taken.

I have always assumed that Cardiff City in 1927 became the only Football Club to take the F.A. Cup out of England as an act of revenge for London taking all the political control out of Wales. That is still today the reason why Cardiff always comes up as a question in sporting Trivial Pursuits quiz-games. Isn't it time for this to change? Never mind the Trivial Pursuits, it's about time that the City of Cardiff became an answer in the Serious Pursuits quiz as well. We can't be a proper Euro-capital if we are still in the Konica League in the political power at our command.